MAKING WORK MATTER

MAKING WORK MATTER

How to Create
Positive Change in Your Company
and Meaning in Your Career

NANCY MCGAW

ROYAL OAK PRESS

To request permission, contact
info@nancymcgaw.com

Paperback ISBN: 979-8-218-35734-4
Ebook ISBN: 979-8-218-35735-1

Design and layout by Sasha Wizansky

Tracy K. Smith, "The Good Life" from *Life on Mars*. Copyright © 2011 by Tracy K. Smith. Reprinted with the permission of The Permissions Company, LLC on behalf of Graywolf Press, Minneapolis, Minnesota, graywolfpress.org.

Royal Oak Press
New York

Dedicated to Robert and Louise

Contents

Introduction

People frequently tell me that they want to have more meaning in their work, to do more than achieve their company's financial goals. They have a bigger vision for the company, one that rests on the conviction that business can contribute to solving some of society's most complex challenges. They want their work to matter.

Many already see opportunities for making changes in their company's products or practices that could benefit people and our planet while contributing to their company's bottom line. But they don't know how to get started or to make the case for change. And they wonder if they are ready to take on the challenge.

If you want to have more impact, this book will help you see possibilities for what to do—and guide you to act as a changemaker in your company. It offers proven skills and strategies. It will also introduce you to people like you who have already taken the leap into what we call *corporate social intrapreneurship*: using the platform of business to tackle urgent social problems and align business and societal value creation.

Before telling you how I came to know these intrapreneurs, I want to share some good news: Companies need your ideas, business acumen, and tenacity more than ever.

Although loud critics are charging companies with practicing "woke" capitalism and disregarding shareholders' interests, forward-looking companies know that managing social and environmental risks and identifying opportunities for value creation in the midst of social and environmental dynamics is critical for achieving long-term success.

To do so, companies will need new products and services, business models, management practices, and bold collaborations. C-suite executives can set the tone, but the change will come only if companies harness the collective imagination and energy of people working in every department of the company—including you.

Can one person actually make a difference? My experience gives me confidence to say yes. Emphatically.

Why am I so sure?

Fifteen years ago, my colleagues at the Aspen Institute Business & Society Program and I set out on a treasure hunt. We believed there were professionals in every industry who longed to do great work and use the platform they had in business to create positive social impact. We wanted to find them.

We sought people who were exceptionally good at their craft and prized by their companies because of their expertise and commitment to their work. But they had to vault over another hurdle as well. They had to be working in a way that created value for their companies, their communities, and the environment. In other words, for example, they had to be creating cool products or services that enhanced the lives of customers, identifying ways to reduce the environmental footprint of their company and its supply chain, or envisioning more inclusive and equitable management practices.

Over the years, this treasure hunt has led us to innovators in some of the largest companies in the world, such as Johnson & Johnson, Walmart, Toyota, McDonald's, and Starbucks, and in technology powerhouses such as Apple, Google, Microsoft, and LinkedIn.

We found them in every department—from finance, R&D, and marketing to strategy, sustainability, and talent management. They were designers, analysts, strategists, business developers, lawyers. Some managed teams; others were individual contributors. Some were far along in their journeys as corporate social intrapreneurs; others were starting out on this path.

At the Aspen Institute Business & Society Program, where I worked, once we started finding these innovators, we believed that we could learn a great deal from working with them and that we could help them be more effective—and courageous—in their commitment to changemaking.

So in 2009, working with a talented design team, I created the Aspen First Movers Fellowship Program. Since then, each year, through a rigorous selection process, we choose about 20 intrapreneurs to become part of the program. To date, we have worked with nearly 300 First Mover Fellows. They have shown that making positive change in large publicly held companies is possible. This book is filled with their stories.

In these pages you will meet people like Kamala Avila-Salmon, a media and marketing expert who is developing inclusive content in motion pictures at Lionsgate; Anupam Bhargava, who launched an eco-friendly engine-cleaning company when he was a general manager at Pratt & Whitney; JoAnn Stonier, who built a global privacy and data protection program at Mastercard; and many more.

These intrapreneurs dare to stand up against prevailing forces arrayed against them. They challenge a system that too often rewards short-term financial gain instead of longer-term results with more widely distributed benefits. Even when they run up against inertia or face resistance, these intrepid innovators persist, achieving small wins that build momentum for deeper change.

Aspen First Mover Fellows consistently tell us that what they have learned in the program and in a community of corporate innovators has transformed their ability to do this work. Along the way, the Fellowship has become one of the world's leading development programs for corporate social intrapreneurs.

I believe thousands of people want to enact this kind of change in their companies and, by doing so, find more meaning in their careers. That is why I wrote this book. I want to bring the lessons we have learned in the First Movers Fellowship Program to a much broader audience and to introduce the strategies we have found to be effective. If you are one of those who long to work in this way, I hope the lessons and the stories from the First Mover Fellows will inspire you to act.

How This Book Is Organized

The First Movers Fellowship Program was built on four key themes, or pillars: innovation, leadership, reflection, and community. We believe all are essential for intrapreneurs to be able to develop the courage and capacity needed to bring innovative ideas to life within companies and to influence change, usually without explicit authority to do so. This book, divided into four sections, integrates these themes throughout so that readers can build the skills and mindsets critical for effective corporate social intrapreneurship.

Section 1 provides guidance for getting started on your journey as a corporate social intrapreneur.

Chapter 1, "Imagine," helps you see possibilities for creating positive change in your company. Seeing opportunities that others may miss or prefer to ignore can ignite your excitement for taking on the challenge of driving change.

Chapter 2, "Discover," emphasizes the importance of defining your personal purpose and thinking about how to align it with your professional endeavors. Knowing what really matters to you is a galvanizing force for action and serves as a shield against the inevitable challenges you will face as an intrapreneur.

Chapter 3, "Reframe," introduces strategies for examining and redefining the social or environmental problem you want to address. It emphasizes that moving to problem-solving too quickly may lead you in the direction of a solution that doesn't work.

The second section of the book offers three essential tools for changemakers.

Chapter 4, "Map," calls on you to take full advantage of your institutional savvy and knowledge of the changing business environment. With that information, you can draw a road map to get from status quo to new possibilities.

Chapter 5, "Seek Small Wins," illustrates the importance of striving to achieve modest strategic victories that take aim at very big problems. Then, creating a narrative around these small wins helps you engage others and build momentum for change.

Chapter 6, "Tell Stories," emphasizes that storytelling is a critical skill for changemakers and offers strategies for improving your storytelling prowess. When you have solid data on problems that you know your organization can address, you may feel that you have an irrefutable case for change. The truth is that you will generate more interest and engagement among colleagues for the change you want to make when you tell compelling stories about how real people have been—or could be—impacted.

Section 3 focuses on creating impactful collaborations.

There is a myth about corporate social intrapreneurs that they are "lone wolves." In fact, corporate change makers do their best work when they make room for others to be part of the change. Chapter 7, "Engage," contains diverse examples of Fellows' successful collaborations and provides strategies for making collaborations work.

Chapter 8, "Inquire," aims to build your capacity for collaboration by showing the importance of shifting away from advocacy for your ideas to curiosity about others' expertise and ideas. And it provides suggestions for crafting questions that will ignite the imaginations of those who could help cocreate solutions to complex problems.

Learning how to be a better listener is the subject of chapter 9, "Listen." It is a skill that most of us think we have mastered. In fact, many of us are careless listeners. Learning how to listen attentively requires practice, but the effort delivers rewards. Listening well, with the intent to learn, is the key to unlocking the value of engaging with others and creating impactful collaborations.

The final section of the book is dedicated to helping you stay the course as an intrapreneur.

Chapter 10, "Dare," addresses a critical inhibitor for many innovators: doubting your own ability to lead the change you want to see. The lessons in the chapter give you confidence and tools to buck conventional wisdom and stand up to opposing forces. You don't have to be innately courageous. The chapter shows that with practice, you can learn how to challenge corporate norms and entrenched practices and advocate powerfully for innovations that make the world better.

Chapter 11, "Reflect," emphasizes the importance of making time to step back from daily routines and consider all of your behaviors and decisions in the context of your aspirations. Reflection is fuel for corporate social intrapreneurs because it builds your self-awareness and helps you link your purpose with your professional endeavors.

Finally, in chapter 12, "Persist," you learn that persistence is an attribute you must bring to the intrapreneurial journey in order to achieve success. There are no shortcuts. But there are victories, and each success gives you wisdom that you can put to use as you face the next challenge on your journey.

Why This Work Matters So Much to Me

Working to help business professionals become effective and courageous corporate social intrapreneurs has highly personal meaning for me. I am dedicated to helping others see possibilities for finding greater meaning in their work than I ever imagined during my tenure in corporate America.

My career didn't begin in an office. It started at the head of a classroom. I was an English major in college and graduated with a teaching certificate. For four years I taught school in the United States and Japan. Quite by chance, I then spent a couple of years working as a consultant in Washington, DC, in health care planning.

I always dreamed of an international career of some kind. (Yes, it was that vague an aspiration.) So I got my master's degree in international relations with a focus on international health and organizations.

As I was finishing graduate school, representatives from banks showed up on campus, and I interviewed with them. I received an offer—which I grabbed. It seemed like an exciting new adventure, although, like so many people who make a career choice they think will be a stepping stone to another pathway, I expected that my days in banking would be relatively few.

Seventeen and a half years later, I was a managing director in a global bank, heading up a portfolio team focused on the chemical industry.

Working with multinational companies (albeit mostly in Toledo and Cleveland rather than in exotic cities around the globe), I learned what it takes to manage complex customer relationships. As a vice president in the shipping division in London in the early 1980s, I saw how hard it was to get money back from clients who were in financial distress. When I looked at the credit approval requests for the loans in arrears, I realized how much we had wanted to believe our cash flow projections and the viability of so-called secondary sources of repayment. Those lessons in hubris and humility have stayed with me. Returning to New York after my stint in shipping, I saw the emergence of leveraged buy-outs and securitizations. I learned how to assess and monitor account profitability and credit exposure. I learned how to cultivate a cold prospect and how to maintain established relationships. I felt the exhilaration of structuring a deal that goes to market. In short, the years were enormously valuable training for understanding how business and the financial markets work.

And yet.

I always felt there was something missing. My unease was reflected in a conversation I had with a vice president on my team. A very capable credit officer, she understood how to manage risk sensibly to address the needs of our colleagues whose objective was to book the business and those of the credit administrators who had to approve the additional credit exposure we incurred. One day, after she returned from maternity leave, she came into my office and closed the door. "I want to do something more meaningful with my career," she said.

So did I, but I thought I was stuck. Not once in my nearly two decades of banking was there ever a conversation about why we did the work we did or whether we could make a difference in society as a whole. We completed annual ethics compliance checklists, but we didn't talk about purpose. We didn't talk about the role that responsible banking practices play in the functioning of an efficient economic system. We knew that managing risk prudently and offering clients a range of services that met their needs served the bank and the client well, but we didn't look beyond those objectives. I would have eagerly participated in such conversations, and I suspect that many of my colleagues would have benefited from them too.

With a deeper sense of why our work mattered to our clients and, more broadly, to the proper functioning of the global economic system, we might have been better and more creative at doing our jobs; and I'm confident that we would have been more deeply engaged in our work.

But I look back now and wonder: Why didn't I ask these questions? Couldn't I have been more creative about finding opportunities at the intersection of business and social value? What held me back? And how could I have helped that competent banker in my office—who left the bank shortly after our conversation—see these opportunities as well?

Coming to the Aspen Institute's Business & Society Program, with its mission of helping business leaders make decisions and investments that align with the long-term health of society, gave me a second chance. Working with corporate social intrapreneurs in the Aspen First Movers Fellowship Program, I now take great satisfaction in knowing that my colleagues and I are helping people in business have the courage and confidence to find meaning in their work and drive positive change in their companies.

By writing this book, I hope to help you find a pathway that brings deeper satisfaction. In short, I aspire to help you make a difference while you are making a living.

I also believe that the world, and more particularly the companies you work for, need your passion, skill, creativity, and determination more than ever. Pernicious social and environmental problems hold us back from the kind of just and equitable society that many of us long for. Business has a critical role to play in tackling those problems. Progress is happening in many companies, and you could nudge it even further.

For all of you who want to take the first step as a corporate social intrapreneur, and for those who are on the path but unsure what to do next, my hope is that this book will serve as a guide.

Beginning

Do not go where the path may lead,
go instead where there is no path
and leave a trail.

—ATTRIBUTED TO RALPH WALDO EMERSON

CHAPTER 1

Imagine Possibilities for Your Company to Create Business and Social Value

Kevin Thompson was working at IBM in 2006 when he read an article by the company's CEO that would change his life. The article by Samuel Palmisano, published in *Foreign Affairs*, argued that multinational corporations were rapidly morphing into globally integrated enterprises, which would transform not only where and by whom goods were produced but also organizational cultures and leadership. Although challenging, Palmisano wrote, this shift "provides an opportunity to advance both business growth and societal progress."[1]

Kevin was a program manager in the corporate citizenship unit. His group didn't have a direct connection to the leadership development programs offered through human resources, but Palmisano's article prompted Kevin to think about how his department could help ensure that IBM had the talent, cultural intelligence, and market knowledge it needed to drive business success and social benefit amid complex global dynamics.

Previously, companies like IBM had used international postings as the training ground for rising executives. These assignments gave them firsthand knowledge of diverse markets and an opportunity to see the company in a global context.

Kevin knew how eye-opening overseas assignments could be. He had spent two years in Ghana as a Peace Corps volunteer, working as an agroforestry manager in a remote village with no running water or electricity.

Although he had been out of the Peace Corps for nearly a decade, the impact was lasting. He had become more resilient, had greater cultural competence, and had a much broader worldview, all qualities that strengthened his ability to lead.

But companies were now sending fewer employees abroad. It was expensive, and companies saw greater advantage in developing local talent within countries. Kevin understood that companies could no longer rely on extended full-time foreign assignments to build the capacity of professionals to manage global enterprises.

So he started to imagine what a shorter-term international placement for IBM employees could look like.

Perhaps, he thought, employees could undertake monthlong assignments in emerging markets with a small team composed of IBM colleagues who came together from different countries. These teams could work closely with organizations in local communities to address high-priority social and environmental challenges in health care, education, sustainability, and economic development. Learning would go both ways. IBM employees would offer their business expertise, and community members would bring their expert knowledge of local issues. Through this engagement, IBMers could gain valuable perspectives on growth markets and have a leadership development experience that would enhance their skills as global citizens and corporate executives.

This idea ultimately became IBM's Corporate Service Corps (CSC).

The CSC is widely applauded now, but all did not immediately embrace it at IBM. "When I first proposed the idea of a program inspired by the Peace Corps at IBM, I was practically laughed out of the conference room," Kevin recalls. For one thing, management asserted that there would be a very limited number of applicants for the program, especially because they would consider offering this opportunity only to the 20 percent of employees deemed to be "high potential." But a question posted on the company intranet about employee interest in new international experiences generated more responses than any CEO post in Samuel Palmisano's tenure. Managers reluctantly agreed to give the program a try.

To their surprise, when the program was launched in 2008, IBM had 14,000 applications from 52 countries for 100 spots. Clearly, the demand was there for a service and leadership experience of this kind. Only three years later, when the company celebrated its centennial, the Corporate Service Corps was identified as one of IBM's 100 "Icons of Progress" that have shaped the past 100 years—in a league with such innovations as the Selectric typewriter and the floppy disk.

More than 15 years after its launch, the CSC has now sent thousands of employees on more than 200 teams to 30 countries. The CSC has also delivered tangible technological, social, and business benefits to the communities where IBMers have worked. Moreover, it has served as an exemplar for many companies that also want to offer their employees a chance to get a global perspective on business and societal challenges and opportunities.

Organizational White Space Is Your Innovation Canvas

Before I met Kevin, I had read Robert Kelley's classic management book, *How to Be a Star at Work*. One of his insights has stayed with me for years. Exceptional performers, he wrote, are "blazing trails in the organization's white spaces."[2] It is an apt metaphor for describing what corporate social intrapreneurs like Kevin do.

Exceptional performers at work see possibilities in that white space for creating the next new thing—some product, service, business model, or business practice that allows a company to outpace its competition.

Corporate social intrapreneurs do that and more. In these white spaces, they imagine innovations that will outrun competitors *and* deliver results that are good for people and the planet. These innovators see beyond short-term financial metrics and believe we need broader measures of business success, ones that integrate social and environmental impacts with financial results.

Peter Drucker, one of the most influential thinkers on business leadership, asserted that every social and global issue of our day is a business opportunity in disguise.[3] Corporate social intrapreneurs see through the disguises to the opportunities for their companies. Finding these opportunities requires vision. Turning the vision into reality requires determination because the work is hard, and there can be pushback from colleagues who see things only as they are, rather than how they could be.

But the tide is turning.

Now Is Your Moment

There is good news for visionaries seeking new ways of doing business that convert problems into opportunities. Public sentiment about the role that business must play in society has shifted. As a result, businesses can no longer thrive by focusing singularly on maximizing value for shareholders. Instead, they must be attentive to a broad range of stakeholders on which their success depends, including employees, customers, suppliers, community members, and the planet.

Businesses must transform—to compete for and retain scarce talent, to meet investor expectations that they will mitigate risks and take advantage of opportunities that arise from environmental and social issues, to become more diverse and inclusive in decision-making, and to comply with a rapidly changing regulatory environment that is setting new standards for action.

This shift was well underway before the COVID-19 pandemic hit and extracted such an enormous toll around the globe. It was well on its way before the murder of George Floyd and the racial reckoning that continues to reverberate. But these crises laid bare the need for transformational change and the critical role that business must play in solving our toughest societal challenges.

The headline from the *2022 Edelman Trust Barometer* report captures the new zeitgeist for companies: "Societal Leadership Is Now a Core Function of Business."[4]

Edelman data show that business outpaces NGOs, government, and media as a trusted institution. However, that level of trust is precarious. Although many companies have made bold commitments to address climate change, economic inequality, workforce reskilling, and other urgent issues, Edelman survey respondents say that business is not doing enough. Companies are beginning to step up, but they have a long way to go to realize their full potential for creating positive change.

That leaves the field wide open for corporate social intrapreneurs who have fresh ideas about how their companies can create value for both the business and society.

Identify the Change That Matters

A starting point for anyone wanting to imagine opportunities in this white space is to ask yourself several overlapping questions: What needs to change in my company to achieve greater positive impact? What is possible to change? What change matters most to me? How can I most effectively use my talent to effect this change?

There are multiple ways to respond to these questions, as you will see in the stories in this chapter and throughout the book.

Linking Leadership Development with Social Impact

In 2006, when Kevin Thompson at IBM began to imagine a way for the corporate citizenship group to support IBM's leadership development efforts, there were few precedents for this kind of collaboration.

Companies offered volunteer opportunities for employees to serve their communities. And companies ran leadership development programs for midlevel and senior executives. But the two existed in parallel universes. Leadership development programs rarely prepared top talent to consider issues beyond the gates of the corporation or to understand the implications of their decisions on society and the planet.

I know this to be true because my first assignment when I joined the Aspen Institute in 2000 was to convene leading thinkers in leadership development—in companies, professional services firms, and academia. We sought answers to two fundamental questions: If we want business to consider its impact on all stakeholders—employees, customers, communities, shareholders, and the planet—what kind of leaders do we need? And how do we develop such leaders?

We searched high and low for exemplary development programs. We found more than a handful of aspirations for such programs but few in place.

That situation is changing now as more leadership programs, both in companies and in business schools, prompt leaders to think deeply about the social impact of business. Nevertheless, there is still plenty of white space for corporate innovators who want to strengthen the connection between social impact and talent management and leadership development.

Creating Structures for Greater Diversity and Inclusion

Over the past few years, many companies have ramped up their commitments to be more diverse, equitable, and inclusive (DEI) organizations. They have hired DEI officers, set staffing goals, donated money, and joined cross-industry pledges. And yet, in many companies results fall way short of rhetoric, and the commitments don't show up in the decisions made about product offerings. So there is still a significant need for innovative corporate change agents, like Kamala Avila-Salmon, to design programs that truly drive change.

Kamala, a marketing expert, has worked in the movie, TV, film, and tech industries. Now, as the first-ever head of inclusive content for the Lionsgate Motion Picture Group, she combines her marketing prowess, love of storytelling, and deep commitment to ensuring that companies produce content that reflects a global audience's diverse perspectives and identities.

Kamala understands that if companies want to produce inclusive content, they must design organizational structures that consistently and powerfully include diverse perspectives.

In her previous job as a senior marketer at Facebook, Kamala saw that Black and Latinx professionals were significantly underrepresented on the marketing team, even though Black and Latinx consumers were heavy users of the Facebook and Instagram platforms. This led to a haphazard process for obtaining diverse views on marketing campaigns, which put an inordinate, unfair burden on employees of color.

"Because there were so few marketers of color," Kamala explained, "some people were constantly being asked to provide feedback on marketing materials and campaigns. For example, they would be asked,

"How do you think this will land with Black consumers?" or "Can you translate this into Spanish for me?" But there was no systematic way to ensure that these perspectives would be considered while campaigns were developed.

"Also, on the other hand," Kamala recalled, "sometimes marketers of color would feel compelled to speak up when they saw something problematic in some of our content. Often this feedback was not well received by the team because they weren't expecting it, and they felt that they were too far down the road to make adjustments. That resistance made marketers of color feel undervalued and disinclined to offer feedback. So Black and Latinx marketers either were being tapped too much for feedback, or found themselves leaning in to provide input that was not appreciated. I knew we needed a different approach."

Under Kamala's leadership, the Facebook marketing team had already created a business resource group called REPRESENT. It gave Black and Latinx marketers an opportunity to network, share insights on career development, serve as a source of support, and consider ways to elevate their voices within the company. Members of REPRESENT underscored the problem of getting randomly asked for advice, often after the fact. It was clear that more structure was needed to ensure that diverse input was intentionally included in developing marketing campaigns.

"I spoke with our chief marketing officer," Kamala recalled, "and said we shouldn't be shipping campaigns to billions of users who represent diverse audiences without being thoughtful about assessing how that campaign will land. And I emphasized that random outreach to Black and Latinx marketers by multiple marketing teams just wasn't enough to meet the need."

So Kamala got the go-ahead to create an Inclusion and Representation Lens Board (IRL) that would serve as a vehicle for providing a cultural competency perspective on all of the company's campaigns.

She put out a call to people from the REPRESENT community, as well as to LGBTQIA, Asian American, Pacific Islander, Indigenous, and disabled marketers and allies at the company, to apply to participate. Through a rigorous application and interview process, Kamala and her team selected board members who were expert marketers and had specific insight into culturally resonant communication by way of their lived identities and experiences.

The Inclusion and Representation Lens Board is now an established part of Facebook's (now Meta's) process for bringing a marketing campaign to life. Review no longer depends on a marketing leader's having the foresight and time to search for different perspectives. Those providing the review have officially opted in to do so, and they are benefiting from their efforts. Board service creates visibility for professionals who might not otherwise be seen. Because the review process is now used across all parts of Meta—for Facebook, Instagram, WhatsApp, etc.—board members interact with leaders across the organization. That puts them on the radar for professional development opportunities and promotions.

The structural changes that Kamala put in place at Facebook, and is introducing now at Lionsgate, also deliver business benefits. Although not designed as a talent retention tool, the IRL Board is helping identify and retain top talent, especially those from historically excluded backgrounds, a critical objective for companies. Moreover, building more cultural competence into marketing campaigns—and now motion picture content—will likely increase customer engagement and revenues.

Expanding Your Customer Base to Reach Underserved Populations

Attracting and retaining customers is key to business success. Most companies are organized around the customer. Marketing, sales, merchandising, and product design departments are all focused on meeting the needs of existing customers and attracting new ones. Still, many social innovators are going beyond the basics and asking: What if we took a broader view of potential customers? In what ways would we need to change our products, services, and business practices to be of service to them?

Innovators in the financial services industry, including many First Mover Fellows, are focused on increasing financial inclusion. Many are trying to make banking accessible for the 30 percent of adults worldwide (6 percent in the U.S.) who are unbanked.

Bringing them into the financial system would enable them to deposit paychecks, get access to credit, and demonstrate the creditworthiness needed to rent an apartment or buy a car. Innovators in this space strive to find ways to remove barriers to banking while developing strategies that are eventually profitable for the firm.

There are many examples from finance, but it is certainly not the only industry with untapped opportunities to serve both business and social interests by expanding the customer base to include people currently excluded from the system.

LinkedIn, for example, has an ambitious mission: to connect the world's professionals to make them more productive and successful. That mission has inspired Gyanda Sachdeva since she joined LinkedIn over a decade ago to work on product development.

In 2015, Gyanda saw that the company was doing a great job connecting professionals to jobs, but it was missing an opportunity to serve a growing number of people who, by choice or circumstance, were working as freelancers in the evolving gig economy.

"The growth of Uber and Lyft may have been the most visible sign of this change," Gyanda explained. "But we knew there was a much bigger need to connect gig workers of all kinds—like graphic designers, accountants, app developers, lawyers—with opportunities for work. Our platform, with its focus on profiling members' educational achievements and work history, wasn't designed to do that."

Although the need and opportunity to serve gig workers was evident to many within LinkedIn, there were competing and compelling priorities, and teams were stretched. "Also," Gyanda recalled, "although we had strong conviction that there was a growth opportunity for us in the freelance market, we had no evidence that would justify allocating the level of resources that would have been required to make significant changes in the LinkedIn app to meet this need."

At the time, resource allocation at LinkedIn was determined on the basis of a "core/strategic/venture" prioritization framework. Building a marketplace for freelancers was considered a "venture bet." So, Gyanda committed to building a prototype separate from the LinkedIn platform. She worked with a small team, including a couple of engineers willing to devote a small percentage of their time to this effort. In 2016, they launched LinkedIn.com/ProFinder.

"The prototype was very basic," Gyanda recalled. "We put as much data as we could from LinkedIn into the experience because we knew that for the product to be successful, we needed to tap into LinkedIn's secret sauce." That sauce is its connection graph: you know someone, I know someone, we know each other, and so on. "These connections are critical for freelancers because they build trust," Gyanda said. "You can reach out to someone who has used a person's services and learn more about the quality of their work."

They designed ProFinder so that freelancers could create profiles that featured their project work. The team also built a workflow process so that someone looking for, say, web development could complete a form describing the services required, send the request to LinkedIn inboxes of web developers whom they thought they might want to work with, and receive up to five proposals from freelancers using ProFinder.

"We stipulated to service providers that if they wanted to be on ProFinder, they had to be willing to respond to requests for proposals within two hours of the time that the request came into their inbox. Constraining the response time created an initial delight factor for the buyer and created a lot of momentum in the early days," Gyanda recalled.

Although ProFinder wasn't yet part of the LinkedIn platform and could be found only by using a search engine like Google, within a few weeks of the launch, hundreds of thousands of freelancers had logged in and received requests for their services.

"At that point, we had more than conviction that the service could connect freelancers with economic opportunities. We had evidence," Gyanda reported. "We also knew that to realize its full potential, the service had to be integrated into LinkedIn's model."

ProFinder functionality has now become embedded in the LinkedIn platform. Freelancers who become members of LinkedIn have the option to self-identify as service providers, and service categories are easily searchable on the platform.

As the gig economy continues to evolve, more work is needed to build this capacity. ProFinder and its successor products have moved from venture territory into a more strategic initiative at LinkedIn. As a result, the company has expanded membership on its main platform, and a growing number of freelance workers have gained access to opportunities.

Addressing Material Risks for Your Industry

Few of us who buy an item of clothing ever think about what it takes to produce it and how that impacts the workforce and the environment. The fact is that the fashion industry faces a host of material social and environmental risks.

Take, for example, the production of jeans, a beloved staple in most of our wardrobes. To produce a pair, you need cotton—and lots of it. Cotton agriculture employs over 300 million people globally. Unfortunately, human rights abuses and damaging environmental practices are the norms on some farms. Second, you need water. Most of us are astonished to realize that the average pair of jeans requires 42 liters of water in the finishing process, and consumers use many more gallons as they repeatedly throw their jeans into the wash. Then, when we discard clothing to pursue the next cool thing, we create a massive waste problem. According to a report from the U.S Environmental Protection Agency, Americans generate 17 million tons of textile waste each year—most of it from discarded shoes and clothing.[5] Over 11 million tons of this waste ends up in landfills.

It was concern about the significant social and environmental risks associated with the fashion industry that prompted Paul Dillinger, VP, head of global product innovation at Levi Strauss & Co., to see new possibilities in corporate white space.

Paul is irreverent, funny, and one of the world's leading experts on denim. He was the first Fulbright Scholar in fashion design and has his master of fine arts from a leading design school in Milan. For many years, Paul climbed the industry ladder working for world-renowned brands. But after five years with one premium brand, he had an aha moment. As he recounted, "I realized I was cutting the same fabric into the same fits using the same finishes, selling them to the same buyers at the large retailers for exactly the same price points with higher margin expectations." He believed he was just making a product more cheaply, which required lower wages for the factory workers who produced the goods.

Disillusioned, he left the industry and accepted a position teaching fashion design at his alma mater, Washington University, intending to imbue the next generation of designers with concern for the planet. Then he got a call from Levi Strauss & Co., a company with a 165-year history and a deep commitment to sustainability.

He agreed to take the role of senior director of color, concept, and design for the Dockers® brand while he continued to teach. Working with the company's sustainability group, he began to design popular styles while also focusing on the environmental and social impacts of producing them.

Under Paul's leadership, Levi Strauss introduced the WellThread™ line of clothing in 2015. Products were based on ethical sourcing standards and designed to look great and wear durably. All the cotton in the garments came from the Better Cotton Initiative, which sets global standards for sustainable production and sustainable livelihoods for cotton farmers and workers. The finishing production processes were redesigned to use far less water. Each product carried a "Care Tag for the Planet" to help consumers learn how to reduce water and energy usage during home care and extend the garment's life.

WellThread now serves as a laboratory for sustainability innovation, Paul told me. "We take a 'research through practice' approach to experimentation and introduce new ideas—material, processes, designs—into the industrial supply chain for small-scale production. We identify challenges early and take risks at scale. We learn a lot from these experiments, and we make mistakes. Then we bring the successful ideas to scale with confidence. The benefit of this approach is that we produce first-to-market, leading innovations."

They also get great press. In May 2021, *Fast Company* presented Levi Strauss & Co. with one of its World Changing Ideas awards, for introducing jeans made from Circulose, a material made from recycled denim. In

2022, Levi Strauss & Co. introduced another breakthrough innovation in its WellThread line. Partnering with Cone Denim, an iconic supplier of denim fabrics since 1891, it developed a custom organic cotton fabric for some products that were dyed with natural indigo, a change that reduced the amount of water and chemicals used in production.

Sparks for Igniting Your Own Imagination for Seeing Opportunities in Corporate White Space

These stories offer a glimpse of the kinds of innovations that First Mover Fellows have championed over the years and suggest the wide range of opportunities you can find to create positive change in your company. Hopefully, these stories and projects will spark your imagination. Below, I offer some tips for finding white space in your own company and blazing into it.

For a deeper dive into possibilities within this white space, I recommend *Changing Your Company from the Inside Out: A Guide for Social Intrapreneurs*, by Gerald Davis and Christopher White. With this book and the pioneering course on corporate social intrapreneurship they created at the Ross School of Business at the University of Michigan, they have become leading experts in the field.[6]

▶ STUDY EXECUTIVE MESSAGES

Kevin Thompson's service in the Peace Corps gave him exceptional insights into how much one can learn from being in a setting that is different from one's own. He gazed into the white space through that lens. However, it was reading the article by his CEO that inspired him to see a shape within that space.

If you want to find an onramp for your own ideas for creating positive change, pay close attention to executive messages. Read the speeches made by your CEO and other top executives. Follow your CEO and other public-facing executives on Twitter, Instagram, and LinkedIn. Listening carefully to leaders when they express passion or interest in certain ideas or activities will help you understand what innovations you are likely to find support for and from whom.

These messages often signal intent but lack specific implementation strategies. That can be your opening.

▶ **READ YOUR CORPORATE REPORTS**

Companies are responding to expectations from investors and the public by disclosing extensive information about their environmental, social, and governance goals and practices. Reading these disclosures will help you find opportunities in your company's white space.

Documents to peruse include the annual report, the 10-K filed with the Securities and Exchange Commission, and your sustainability/ESG report. In addition, some companies disclose their DEI goals in the sustainability report or a separate document.

When I was a banker, I spent far more time reading my customers' public documents than my own. I figured I worked in the business every day and knew it from the inside out. In fact, I didn't. Now, as companies disclose even more information, you will likely find hidden gems in these documents.

It can feel like a daunting task. After all, you have a day job. But you don't have to master all the content in these published reports. Focus on answering a couple of essential questions. For example: (1) What are the risks that affect your business? (2) What parts of the world are most important for your company? (Make sure you know where you are generating your revenues, where you are sourcing raw materials. If you are in the manufacturing business, learn where you are producing goods sold.) (3) What commitments has your company made to becoming more sustainable, equitable, and diverse? To make the search more relevant to your own interests, create your own short list of questions to guide your exploration.

▶ **KNOW THE MATERIAL RISKS FOR YOUR INDUSTRY**

Using the SASB Standards is one starting point to assess your industry risks. SASB, the Sustainability Accounting Standards Board, developed its Standards in consultation with companies and industry groups. The SASB Standards show you what experts have determined are the social and environmental factors that are most likely to be material to your industry. You may be surprised by what you find. For example, is product packaging a material risk for companies in your industry? How about data security and customer privacy? Fair labor practices? Accident and safety management? Once you have identified the material factors for your company, you can explore how your company is addressing them. There may be a way for you to imagine new approaches for mitigating social and environmental risks that could have a material, long-term impact on your company's success. You can explore the SASB Standards using the Materiality Finder at SASB.org, where you can also download the Standards for your industry.

▶ STUDY YOUR COMPETITORS

Once you have a handle on the material social and environmental risks for your industry, figure out how your competitors are mitigating them. Learn what goals they have set and what progress they are making toward achieving them. Their sustainability reports can provide an overview. The best of these reports present data about how companies are managing material environmental, social and governance (ESG) factors. Compare their metrics against the ones established in your own company.

The bigger challenge, and one that will require more ongoing research on your part, is to look beyond your competitors' risk management practices to understand how they are creating value by leaning into social and environmental trends that will impact their business— and most likely yours as well. Select a couple important competitors and scrutinize their public reports and analyst presentations to see if you can answer a variety of questions, such as: Are they developing new products or services that are "greener" or more inclusive than ones previously on offer? Do you see evidence that they are rethinking their business models in fundamental ways that take social and environmental factors into account? Are there innovative protocols in place to bring in diverse stakeholder perspectives to help shape decision making for future success? Then you can ask yourself if your company is keeping pace. If not, there may be an opening for you to step up to be a champion for change.

▶ HAVE COFFEE WITH COLLEAGUES

You can learn a great deal from your colleagues. As companies respond to the changing expectations of employees, investors, customers, and regulators to step up to their potential to create a positive impact on society and the planet, more and more employees are becoming involved in these efforts. Members of corporate finance and controller teams, for example, are working with sustainability teams to meet new disclosure and assurance requirements. Employee resource groups are speaking up about the well-being of workers. Human resources teams are rethinking performance metrics to embed sustainability and DEI achievements. The list goes on. Meeting regularly with your colleagues across the organization and asking questions will allow you to gain insights into these new alliances and see where more innovation is needed.

▶ BE INTENTIONAL ABOUT BEING INSPIRED

Corporate social intrapreneurs don't wait to be inspired. Instead, they are on the lookout for possibilities.

I reflect now on my years in banking and realize that I had tunnel vision. I didn't look up often enough from my immediate responsibilities to spot trends coming over the horizon. As a result, although I wanted to feel more personally fulfilled, it didn't occur to me that if I looked at my work with a wider lens, I might see opportunities for making a difference that would have infused my work with more meaning.

I know now that effective corporate social intrapreneurs stay tuned in to these trends and seek opportunities to use their expertise and their passion to make a difference.

There are endless ways to step up as a corporate social intrapreneur if you travel in a "universe of possibility." In this universe, so compellingly described in Rosamund Stone Zander and Benjamin Zander's *The Art of Possibility,* you move beyond a "world of measurement" where notions of scarcity and peril constrict your options. In a universe of possibility, you see opportunities that others don't, and you are willing to dare to innovate. The Zanders describe a mindset that, I believe, illuminates the approach that corporate social intrapreneurs bring to their work. "When you are oriented to abundance," they write, "you care less about being in control, and you take more risks. You may give away short-term profits in pursuit of a bigger dream; you may take a long view without being able to predict the outcome. In the measurement world, you set a goal and strive for it. In the universe of possibility, you set the context and let life unfold."[7]

The need to turn problems into possibilities for change propels corporate social intrapreneurs on their quests. The ability to imagine opportunities that others miss drives them to act. A deep sense of possibility and purpose keeps them on the journey. With that mindset, they find the white space where business and social value can emerge. In the next chapter, we'll look at how corporate social intrapreneurs develop and hold on to that mindset.

Purpose is not a goal to be set. It is not something we create. It is not some "great idea" we come up with. It is something we discover. Purpose is there all the time, and it's waiting for us.

—KEVIN CASHMAN, *LEADERSHIP FROM THE INSIDE OUT: BECOMING A LEADER FOR LIFE*

CHAPTER 2

Discover Your Purpose to Fuel
Your Commitment to Change

Since the beginning of the First Movers Fellowship Program, we have prompted Fellows to think more deeply about what their purpose is and how to access it more fully in their personal and professional lives. We firmly believe that getting clear about personal purpose will boost their efforts to see opportunities for change that others miss. It also serves as a bulwark against disappointment and discouragement and helps them stay the course in championing change, even when forces supporting the status quo are arrayed against them.

Being guided by purpose accrues other benefits to all of us, not just to corporate change makers. "When you get clarity of purpose," Nick Craig, author of *Leading from Purpose*, writes, "you see the world through a unique filter, and this gives you the opportunity to be much more creative and innovative about how you lead in your life."[1]

In addition, it enhances personal well-being. In 2020, as the COVID-19 pandemic raged, McKinsey researchers found that people who said they were "living their purpose" at work reported levels of well-being that were five times higher than those of people who weren't.[2] The report referenced other findings that demonstrated the health benefits of purposeful living—including greater longevity and less risk of dementia or stroke.

For all these reasons, we believe that discovering and articulating your purpose is time well spent and offers lasting rewards. That is why we thread purpose exploration throughout the First Movers Fellowship experience.

We ignite the process during a session that takes place one evening in the first seminar. We sit around a campfire (in person where possible, online when necessary) and ask Fellows to tell a personal story in response to this prompt.

One could say a key task in life is to discover and define our life purpose, and then accomplish it to the best of our ability. We invite you to share a single, specific story of a moment, or period of time, where your purpose became clearer to you. For example, a moment where your calling happened, where there was an important awakening or teaching, where there was a special experience or event, or where you received some guiding vision.

For 15 years, with other Fellows and members of the design team, I have listened as Fellows have told their extraordinary stories. We have laughed and cried and felt profoundly moved by the stories and by the privilege of having the opportunity to bear witness to these reflections.

Our commitment to every Fellow is that all conversations in the Fellowship are off the record, but I have reached out to three Fellows who have given me permission to share their purpose stories in the hope that they may be useful to you. Following these stories, I offer strategies you can use to discover (or uncover) your purpose so that it can guide you—at work and at home.

Marika's Story: Acting on Inequality

Marika McCauley Sine lived abroad as a child, moving between her home state of Hawaii and Indonesia and Sri Lanka, as her parents worked in international development. While living in Sri Lanka as a high schooler, she found herself increasingly aware of the pervasive poverty in her neighborhood in the capital city of Colombo.

"Every day as I was driven to school," Marika recalled, "we would pass by a woman begging on the sidewalk with her child, just 20 yards away from my comfortable home. I began to feel vividly the incongruity and injustice in the gap between her circumstances and mine."

Spurred by this experience, she decided to study more about and try to act to address the drivers of poverty. She began volunteering for microcredit programs for women in Colombo, and in college she studied international relations with a focus on development economics and women's studies. After college, she joined AmeriCorps, which led to a role at Oxfam, a global organization dedicated to ending poverty and injustice. Her job was in Vietnam, working in the Mekong Delta to study the impact of the worldwide boom in shrimp consumption on smallholder farmers in Vietnam. High prices for shrimp were prompting experienced rice farmers to shift to shrimp farming, but it required specialized expertise and capital. Many lost their livelihoods in this shift and were pushed deeper into poverty.

There, Marika had another insight that further fueled her sense of purpose. "I saw the great work that nonprofit organizations were doing to help farmers transition to new income sources," she explained. "I also saw large multinationals working with the same communities to provide significant, specialized training as farmers started their new enterprises—which benefited the companies as well, as they'd ultimately purchase the shrimp. I was intrigued by the power at the intersection of business and community benefits."

She then sought to build her expertise in the emerging field of sustainable business by seeking a graduate degree at the Harvard Kennedy School. Marika arrived just as Harvard established its first Corporate Responsibility Initiative, and she and a friend started a club for students with common interests. It became the most popular club on campus that year. "Then," she said, "I had a unique opportunity to take on a summer internship with the Coca-Cola Company, a sponsor of the initiative."

Given her nonprofit roots, she was initially skeptical of taking on a role in a global business. "I remember thinking that I would take this internship to learn, but that I would ultimately look for a job more strongly linked to my purpose, which I assumed would be outside of business."

As it turned out, her first assignment was helping design a plan to address the risk of child labor in Coca-Cola's sugarcane supply chain in El Salvador. She observed yet again the powerful potential that business could have as a force for good in vulnerable communities. "I realized that

I could work in business and have a positive impact." After graduating, she accepted a job in the company's sustainability team and ended up staying for 10 years.

At Coca-Cola, Marika championed a number of innovations, including a program with a goal of enabling the economic empowerment of five million women entrepreneurs across the company's value chain by 2020. "For the first time, we wanted to offer women running small-scale retail businesses selling our products access to practical business skills training, financial services, and connections with peers and mentors so that they could increase their incomes and boost their capabilities as businesswomen," Marika told me. By 2020, Coca-Cola and its partners had met and exceeded their goal, enabling the economic empowerment of over six million women across 100 countries and territories. Building on these experiences, Marika has continued her career in sustainability to this day.

Andy's Story: Learning from Ancient Wisdom

Andy Toung grew up in a three-generation household, with grandparents who immigrated to the U.S. from Taiwan. All generations were fans of books and films that featured Taiwanese martial arts heroes.

"So it's not surprising that I grew up studying various forms of martial arts," Andy said. "I was particularly fascinated with tai chi, often referred to as 'meditation in motion,' because of the philosophy behind it around balance and change. Its focus on the complementary forces of yin and yang reminds us that something that seems positive now can turn into a negative and vice versa. That philosophy makes so much sense when you sit back and observe life with its polarities and dualities. Many people only see the combat element of the martial arts, but these ancient practices are actually deeply meditative. It is that mental aspect of learning tai chi that has fascinated me for a very long time and guided my path."

In addition to studying martial arts, Andy had a curiosity as a young boy that was fueled by exposure to the world of tech, space travel, and finance, partly due to his mother's interest in investing and her work at a company that supported the space shuttles.

He continued to pursue tai chi and other interests at Stanford University, where he earned bachelor's and master's degrees in management science and engineering. A few years into his career at a California venture capital firm, he was asked to open an office in Hong Kong.

Andy began to ponder the kind of impact that he hoped to make in his life and whether he wanted to continue to work in the financial industry. He thought about his long-standing commitment to self-improvement and to understanding the choices that people made to do better in all aspects of their lives. Then his expertise in tai chi, his connection to master teachers in these ancient arts, his location in Asia, and his language skills opened another door.

He was offered the job of chief of staff for Jet Li, the famous Chinese film actor and martial arts master. (Some know Jet Li for his starring roles in Chinese films. Others may remember his performances in American movies, including *Romeo Must Die* and *Lethal Weapon 4*.)

"As I thought about this opportunity," Andy recalled, "I remembered a quote that goes something like this: 'There are two ways to cast light in the world. One is to be the candle; the other is to be the light that reflects it.' It seemed to me that Jet Li was a pretty big candle. So I accepted the offer to move to Beijing and manage his personal, philanthropic, and commercial projects."

That choice soon led to another opportunity that took Andy closer to work that mattered deeply to him. In 2011, he was asked to work with Jet Li and Jack Ma, a Chinese entrepreneur, to establish Taiji Zen, a lifestyle company with the mission of spreading "Health and Happiness for All." In his role as general manager and corporate board member, Andy could pursue his passion for bringing the wisdom of ancient Chinese arts to the public.

When it was time for Andy to return to the U.S., he faced a crossroads. Initially, he hoped to establish Taiji Zen centers in the U.S. That plan didn't materialize, but another opportunity appeared on the horizon. Classmates from Stanford had started a new company, Gusto, a human resources platform for payroll, benefits, hiring and onboarding, and other services. He signed on as the start-up's CFO.

That choice may seem like a significant departure from his interest in providing opportunities for people to achieve greater health and well-being. In fact, it was directly in line with this purpose.

Gusto's mission is to make work meaningful for everyone, everywhere. (It's revealing that in the company's earliest days, it was called Zen Payroll.) "I saw that this company could make a huge difference in people's lives," Andy explained. "Gusto's 200,000 customers, mostly small and medium-sized enterprises, are the fountainhead for wealth creation for thousands of Americans."

Today, Gusto processes tens of billions of payroll dollars annually and enables companies to deliver employee benefits like health insurance and retirement accounts. And their services are evolving as needs emerge. In the wake of the pandemic, Gusto developed platforms that support remote work and helped companies pay contractors in 80 countries and register as a business in all 50 states and Washington, DC.

Now, as chief strategy officer at Gusto, Andy works with colleagues to explore how they can more effectively measure the company's social impact on employers and employees across three key pillars: enhancing peace of mind, fostering great places to work, and increasing personal prosperity.

Meanwhile, Andy has expanded his training in the martial arts to include jujitsu, and he brings lessons from this training to work and to his family life every day: practicing patience, listening, managing energy, and finding the right balance of efficiency and sensitivity in business and his personal interactions.

John's Story: Improving Financial Health for All

"Years ago," John Thompson recalled, "I had just gotten my dream assignment, the one I felt I had been destined for. I was named chief information officer in the brokerage business unit at H&R Block in Kansas City."

His job was to build the systems that would enable H&R Block to cross-sell financial services to its taxpaying customers. Trained as a computer scientist, John had moved up fast to this position. But he soon made a startling discovery that threatened to derail his effort. Some 75 percent of H&R Block's customers earned less than $35,000 a year, and almost 65 percent of them didn't have a bank account. "I realized that the notion of trying to sell stocks, bonds, equities, mutual funds, and insurance to this customer base was ridiculous," John said. "These were products these clients could not possibly afford and didn't understand."

He was determined to figure out how customers managed their financial resources, including income tax refunds. He learned that many of them didn't have accounts at commercial banks, so they had to rely on alternative providers like retail operations for cashing their checks and on pawnshops and payday lenders to borrow money. "These providers," John said, "took unfair advantage of customers by charging high fees and limiting access to services." At that moment, his personal purpose became much clearer to him.

He pledged to do something about these inequities. "My team and I figured that if we redeployed the technology and the personnel within our reach, we could do things differently. Within H&R Block we built electronic banking systems, started a bank, and began to focus the company on the success of the underserved customer." However, organizational changes made it impossible for him to continue to pilot bold initiatives from his current position. To continue this work, which he cared so deeply about, John had to leave his coveted CIO job and take a position within the company that was, in effect, a considerable demotion.

As John recalled, "With this change, I had no job description. I had no job, really, other than I was going to try to build some financial services stuff for the tax business." What he did have was a passion for offering appropriate and responsible financial services to an underserved customer base.

His new boss offered support and pushed John not just to use his technical skill but to get outside the office, and even the company, and learn. For John, it was a complete eye-opener. "I was a computer programmer. I had no idea how clients with incomes below $35,000 managed their finances, but what I found is that the clients we were trying to serve were some of the most intelligent, capable, articulate, inventive people that I had ever met, and that was a real inspiration."

Since then, John has not stopped learning and has redoubled his commitment to deliver products and services that meet the needs of people who have historically been neglected by financial services companies. He eventually left H&R Block and started an organization that worked with tax preparation companies so they could better serve their clients who depended heavily on the annual tax refunds they got from the government. He then became an executive at the Financial Health Network, a nonprofit authority on consumer financial well-being.

In 2021, John came full circle. He was recruited back to H&R Block to serve as vice president of financial services, responsible for overseeing the kinds of customer services he began to imagine early in his career. "Already," he told me, "we've built no-cost, no-minimum-balance, no-overdraft checking accounts to help people receive and spend their money, even if they don't have high balances. We offer automated budgeting tools and products to help people build emergency savings. And more products are in development that will help customers accumulate savings for retirement and help them monitor and restore damaged credit."

The headline on John's LinkedIn profile reflects the purpose that has been central to his work all these years: Improving financial health for all.

Uncovering Your Own Purpose

Like Marika, Andy, and John, all of us have a purpose that defines us and gives direction to our lives. However, sometimes our sense of purpose gets buried in our daily routines. When that happens, the choices we make at home and at work may not be aligned with what matters most to us.

To keep purpose front and center in the choices we make, we must set intentions to discover, review, or rediscover our purpose regularly. Only then can we determine whether the work we are doing is truly connected to that purpose.

As I wrote earlier in this chapter, we prompt Fellows to reflect on their purpose by asking them to tell a story around a campfire, and I am always moved by the responses I hear when we ask Fellows: When did your life's purpose become visible to you?

Nevertheless, no matter how much I love the question and how inspired I am by hearing the stories of others, I confess that I personally find the question intimidating. My inclination is to waffle, to say that

I'm not really sure what my purpose is. If I'm honest, my initial response frightens me into thinking I may not have one.

I have come to understand that few of us have a ready-made answer to questions about purpose. Discovering our purpose and living it fully in our lives is a process, not a single exercise. Sometimes there are lightning-bolt moments, but most of us need to commit to being mindful and intentional throughout our lives to check in on what we believe our purpose to be.

Bill George, former CEO of Medtronic and executive fellow at Harvard Business School, who writes extensively on authentic leadership, provides more context and reassurance for those of us who find it hard to pinpoint our purpose. He writes about the importance of discovering your "true north," which he defines as "your orienting point—your fixed point in a spinning world—that helps you stay on track as a leader."[3]

Only by discovering your true north, he asserts, can you live into your potential to be a leader. But here is the good news—for me, at least. George says that finding your true north is hard work and may take years. I take comfort in knowing that even for an accomplished leader like Bill George, and for the 175 others he profiled in *Discover Your True North*, clarity about purpose didn't happen overnight.

Also, I have learned that it is important to recognize that your sense of purpose at age 25 can be quite different from your definition of purpose at 40. One moment can be transformative. The joyous arrival of a child or the profound sadness of a loss can prompt us to recalibrate. In fact, examining these pivotal experiences is central to realizing purpose. But all of that discovery takes time and intent, and it's important to find a path to discovery that works best for you.

Here are some ideas to get you started.

▶ IDENTIFY YOUR VALUES

I love the purpose exploration story told by one of my colleagues at the Aspen Institute, Simran Jeet Singh, who runs the Aspen Religion and Society Program. In his moving book *The Light We Give: How Sikh Wisdom Can Transform Your Life*, he recalls a spring break during his childhood when his parents invited Larry Mills, a leadership coach, to come to their house to guide the family through a process by which they would prepare a document that articulated their family's mission, vision, and shared values.

Simran and his brothers resisted giving up any of their precious spring break, but finally they agreed to meet this coach when their parents astutely highlighted Mills's career as a leadership trainer for the San Antonio Spurs, the boys' favorite basketball team. They eagerly anticipated hearing stories of some of the players they admired. Little did they know what was in store for them.

After two long days of deep inquiry, Simran's family completed a mission statement that reflected their collective values. As he writes, "My brothers and I participated in this process that weekend out of respect for our parents and Mr. Mills. I had no idea then that this single exercise would serve me for years to come. Two decades later, I still consult it almost daily as I work through decisions."[4] Few of us can recall spring breaks that delivered that much meaning.

Identifying the values that matter the most to you is a productive starting point for a purpose-discovery process. As Simran learned, this exercise is more difficult than you think, especially if you limit yourself to a very small number of the values that you hold most dear. You will need to revise the list multiple times before it feels right.

Brené Brown insists that the maximum number of core values you should have is two. In her "Living into Our Values" workshops, participants consider a list of more than 80 values—from accountability to wisdom—and she suggests they start by circling the 10 to 15 that resonate most with them. Then, they must keep reflecting until they whittle their list down to the two values that "are the most important and dear to you, that help you find your way in the dark, that fill you with a sense of purpose."[5]

She also makes the point, since many people ask, that there should be no difference between your personal and professional values. "We don't shift our values based on context," she writes. "We are called to live in a way that is aligned with what we hold most important regardless of the setting or situation."

This values-identification process, she says, is a building block for becoming a more daring leader. It is also, I believe, a stepping stone for getting clarity on your purpose.

▶ EXPLORE YOUR PAST

Nick Craig, who runs a leadership company that helps people discover their purpose and examine their impact, advises participants in his seminars to mine their past experiences for clues about their purpose.

For example, he invites participants to reflect on "magical moments" from their childhood. "When we evoke strong and powerful childhood memories in ourselves, we reexperience the moments of wonder and insight that are the basic ingredients of purpose."[6] Craig suggests describing these childhood moments in detail and thinking about why the experience was so meaningful and how you felt in that moment.

He also suggests looking back to recall "crucible stories" in your life, the darkest or most discouraging moments. In these experiences you were tested. Think carefully about what happened. How did you feel? What did you do? And, perhaps most important, what did you learn about yourself through the experience? Do these lessons provide insights about how you might define your purpose?

Another approach is to look back on some of the most significant choices you have made in your life and in your career. Make a short list of these choices and then ask yourself: In each choice, what guided my decision? Did purpose play a role? If so, how? Are there choices I have made when purpose played no role—or when I may have made a choice that felt uncomfortable based on who I understood myself to be? What happened then and why?

It is also helpful to ask: When have I felt most alive, most fulfilled? What was I doing in those moments? Why was the experience so impactful? What would I have to do now to bring that level of engagement into my work and my personal life again?

▶ FIND YOUR KEYSTONE QUESTION

More advice for finding purpose comes from Hal Gregersen, in his book *Questions Are the Answer: A Breakthrough Approach to Your Most Vexing*

Problems at Work and in Life. Gregersen believes that becoming aware of our personal "keystone question" can provide guidance throughout life.

Such questions, he explains, are the ones "we ask of ourselves in the attempt to be our best selves."[7] The impact of finding the one that resonates with you can be transformative.

In his book, he relates his own quest to find the question that guides his path. As a child, he was exposed to emotional abuse. To cope, he grew up constantly asking himself, "What can I do to keep my father—and, by extension, everyone around me—happy?" That question dogged him for decades until he faced exhaustion and a health emergency that prompted him to reflect and recalibrate. He then realized that he had let the wrong question take hold of his life, and it was time to rethink. The keystone question for him today is "How can I make a positive difference in this person's life right now?"[8]

It might seem like a subtle change, but, he writes, "it pushes me toward a version of happiness that doesn't assign me responsibility for others' happiness."

You may find that searching for your own keystone question ignites your imagination more quickly than seeking an answer to a quest for purpose.

▶ CREATE YOUR OWN "CAMPFIRE" EXPERIENCE

Identifying your values, examining crucible experiences in your life, or finding your keystone question requires that you spend time in quiet reflection. (I offer strategies for developing your own reflection practices in chapter 11.) Tackling the challenge requires vulnerability and a willingness to wrestle with your thoughts and realize that there may be a disconnect between what really matters to you and how you are living your life at present.

Because the process can feel uncomfortable and even daunting, you may be inclined to set the task aside for another, more convenient time.

Does delay matter? Tim Urban, an exemplary storyteller and self-proclaimed master procrastinator, says yes and explains why. In his funny and memorable TED Talk, "Inside the Mind of a Master Procrastinator," which has been viewed over 60 million times, he argues that procrastinating on tasks that have a deadline really doesn't matter so much because procrastinators usually get the job done when a deadline looms. The greater challenge for most of us, he explains, is putting off taking action on situations in our lives that are not deadline driven: things like exercising, sustaining relationships, eating healthy meals, spending time with friends and family, and, I would add, discovering our unique purpose. This kind of procrastination, he posits, can be a source of unhappiness and regret that make us feel like "spectators in our own lives."[9]

Indeed, there is a consequence to letting your days slip by without intentional inquiry into what matters most to you. As Annie Dillard reminds us in *The Writing Life*, "How we spend our days is, of course, how we spend our lives."[10]

Socrates, the Greek philosopher, was even more direct: "The unexamined life is not worth living."

The philosophers agree. If we don't challenge ourselves to think about what matters most to us, we may squander our opportunities to live our lives fully and make a difference.

So resolve today to create your own campfire-like experience. Don't wait to feel ready. Set aside 30 minutes to get started. Grab a journal and a pen. Perhaps sketch a campfire in the margin of your blank page. Then choose two or three questions to prompt reflection. You can start with the one we ask Fellows: to think of a time when purpose became clear to you—or you can select a couple of questions that will help you interrogate your life so far. Return to the journal as often as you need until you feel you have a statement that resonates.

Then check in on your purpose periodically to make sure it is serving you—and you are serving it.

If I had an hour to save the world,
I would spend 55 minutes defining the problem
and five minutes finding solutions.

—ATTRIBUTED TO ALBERT EINSTEIN

CHAPTER 3

Reframe the Problem
You Want to Solve

James Inglesby, raised in South Africa and trained as a chemical engineer in the United Kingdom, joined Unilever in 2010. Early on, he won an excellence award for achieving energy efficiencies in one of Unilever's margarine factories. Unilever then assigned him to the new-business unit, a small group charged with looking for new, sustainable business opportunities that could deliver value in 5 or 10 years. In particular, he was expected to look for business opportunities for "base of the pyramid" customers in emerging markets—i.e., four billion people around the globe who earn less than $2 per day.

What really worried James were toilets—or rather the lack of them. James came to realize that over two billion people did not have access to proper sanitation. In many urban areas, at any time of the day or night, if citizens have to relieve themselves, they must walk to the public facilities, buy a ticket to enter the toilet, and then wait in line for their turn. Generally, these toilets are dirty and unsafe.

James was determined to use his platform at Unilever to tackle this problem and perhaps develop a new market opportunity for Unilever's cleaning products. In 2012, as Unilever's representative, he began working with NGOs, government authorities, and IDEO in Kumasi, Ghana, to find a way to provide affordable sanitation services to hundreds of residents of this city. Together they founded Clean Team Ghana, a sanitation business serving the urban poor.[1]

Their business model was straightforward. For a monthly fee that was less than what a family might typically pay for using public toilets, the Clean Team would provide households with an attractive portable toilet to place in their homes. Each toilet would be fitted with a removable insert to collect waste. Households would contract with the organization to have a service team come to the house two or three times per week to collect used inserts and install a cleaned one. The service team would take the waste to a central processing facility. Inserts would be cleaned and the waste transported to the municipal treatment site.

After months of work finding a model toilet, negotiating with municipal agencies to dispose of the waste, and hiring the Clean Team, the pilot program began. It appeared to be a popular service.

Then came bad news. Revenues were insufficient to cover expenses. Some members of the team that had designed the pilot were quick to point to poverty as the culprit. Impoverished households, they argued, could not afford these services.-

Further investigation, however, told a different story. The problem was not that customers wouldn't or couldn't pay. Instead, service team members had not been adequately trained and incentivized to collect payments. Team members assigned to collect the fees didn't know how to ask for payments or establish reliable records. Nor did they understand that their success in collecting the payments would have a direct impact on their compensation. Once the organization provided this training and tweaked the incentive system, the financial situation quickly improved.

Avoid Solving the Wrong Problem

Most of us love to solve problems. And in business, problem-solving is a highly valued skill. Successful business professionals are rewarded for getting to the answers. They analyze gaps and take steps to bridge them.

Corporate social intrapreneurs are driven to fix some of the world's most vexing problems—poverty, environmental injustice, climate change, and, as in James Inglesby's case, poor sanitation. These intrapreneurs bring laudable energy to finding solutions. However, before our Fellows get too far down the solutions path, we urge them to interrogate and redefine the problem itself. Without taking the time for this critical step, they could easily waste time working on solutions that don't achieve the results they seek.

Had Clean Team Ghana gone with its initial diagnosis—that the community could not afford this service or prioritize payment for it—the group might have determined that the pilot had failed and ceased delivering the service. Instead, they built training into the business model for the service providers and changed the equation.

We offer First Movers a tool kit of strategies, described below, for successfully reframing problems. In seminars, we invite them to test out these strategies to see if they produce new insights about the problems they want to solve.

▶ SEEK MULTIPLE PERSPECTIVES

One important lesson in the Clean Team story is that reframing often requires a collective effort. Our interpretation of any problem is limited by our own perspective. For most of us, misalignment on problem definition happens in ways large and small more frequently than we may realize.

For example, think of a disagreement you have had recently with a colleague or loved one. Your teammate hasn't completed an assignment on time, for example. You think she has dropped the ball, but she says you didn't clearly communicate the full scope of the task. Your teenager arrives home after curfew. You think he is being defiant. He explains that he chose to drive a friend home who had been drinking. Without taking time to understand how the teammate or child sees the problem, you might head toward a solution that is inadequate or, in these cases, unjust.

The wicked social and environmental problems that social intrapreneurs want to address offer multiple layers of complexity that require careful interrogation.

Take the challenge of expanding economic opportunity for low-income workers, families, and communities. Abigail Carlton is an expert in this field. For nearly a decade, she led initiatives at the Rockefeller Foundation to expand opportunities, put people to work, and create more inclusive markets. In 2018, seeing the incredible potential that the for-profit sector had for making a difference in this space, she took her expertise into the world of business.

She became the first head of social impact at Indeed, a company so committed to expanding opportunities for individuals looking for work that it has pledged to help 30 million job seekers facing barriers to find jobs by 2030. However, when she arrived, she found that while senior executives were determined to use the Indeed job search platform to make a difference, many of them didn't fully grasp the nature of the problems faced by the population they sought to serve.

To learn more before designing products to address this market need, Abigail created a volunteer experience that allowed executives to work directly with job seekers and organizations that helped them overcome barriers to employment.

"We arranged for executives to sit next to job seekers having trouble finding work," Abigail recalled. "They worked with them on their résumés and helped them develop an elevator pitch and prepare for an interview. This hands-on experience gave executives a deeper understanding of the challenges these individuals faced. It was eye-opening to learn how lack of housing, training, transportation, or childcare inhibited job searches. They also gained an appreciation for the tenacity and skill these individuals used to navigate the constraints they faced."

These executives also met with leaders in grassroots organizations that have assisted job seekers for years to get a deeper appreciation for the kind of support needed to help people land a job and remain in the workforce.

"The impact of these volunteer experiences has been significant," Abigail reported. "Our leaders saw more clearly the connections between our social impact commitment and what we do as a business. It was an inflection point in our journey toward putting equitable hiring at the center of our work. Today, our commitment to society is a core pillar of Indeed's business strategy. While this experience wasn't the sole reason for that shift, in important ways it set the table for many conversations that followed."

All of us can learn a great deal by understanding how others interpret or experience a given challenge. It's easy to do, but we often skip this step.

To begin, create a list of stakeholders and other individuals whose opinion you value, and seek their perspective on the problem. Compare their definitions of the problem with your own. You may be surprised by what you learn, and these lessons may prompt you to rethink the problem you seek to solve.

▶ ASK WHY FIVE TIMES

When someone has offered their perspective, then, with the persistence of a two-year-old, ask, "Why?" "Why are there so few minority suppliers in our supply chain?" "Why aren't our products working for all of our potential customers?" "Why do we have such a negative environmental footprint?" Then challenge the first answer to the question by asking "Why?" again. Keep going! Asking Five Whys is a time-honored approach to root-cause analysis. By the time you have gotten responses from several people to multiple "why" questions, you will certainly have a much more nuanced view of the problem that could put you on a different problem-solving path than you originally envisioned.

Ashley Lykins took this approach when she was guiding corporate responsibility for the JPMorgan Chase Foundation across 16 markets in Asia Pacific. One of her responsibilities was to develop programs that would support educational advancement for children in the region. However, to do so, she and her team realized that they first needed to deal with the problem of children being absent from the classroom.

As Ashley recalled, "Before I began to design programs to address the need, I sought extensive input from teachers, parents, children, and community members. I didn't stop with the first response to key questions like 'Why are there gaps in the educational advancement of some children? What are the barriers that are keeping children from attending school?' I continually asked why to each response, to dive more deeply to gain more understanding of the problem."

They learned that a lack of clean water and sanitation lay at the heart of the problem. Illness was keeping children at home.

After reframing the problem, Ashley and the team designed a program that had no obvious relationship to education. They worked with partners, including *Sesame Street*, to build awareness of the importance of hygiene and handwashing, which improved the health of children and families and eventually led to more consistent school attendance.

▶ **APPLY CONSTRAINTS**

It may seem counterintuitive, but another strategy for problem reframing is to impose constraints. It's tempting to think that it is best to keep all options open when you are solving a problem, but narrowing the boundaries often leads to new insights.

To show how constraints can drive breakthrough thinking and galvanize action, we simply have to look to our experiences during the pandemic. We all improvised and innovated in the midst of the lockdowns and anxiety. Facing massive constraints, companies also, with lightning speed, modified human resources practices, collaboration strategies, product offerings, and supply chains practices in ways they would have found unimaginable before COVID-19 disrupted our world.

An illustrative example comes from Tang Industries, a privately held diversified holding company with operations throughout North and South America and in Asia, when it was called on to help meet the dire need for personal protective equipment.

Tang Industries processes steel and aluminum and recycles and trades aluminum and scrap metal. "Our business is essentially to sell metal widgets," Patrick Liang, a managing director at the company and a First Mover, explained. "On occasion, however, we have used our sourcing capabilities to meet customer and vendor requests for some other rather oddball items. So it wasn't surprising that in the crazy early days of the pandemic, many of our customers reached out to us to try to buy medical masks because they knew we had sourcing operations in China. We were overwhelmed with orders."

Patrick's colleagues initially approached the problem as they did for other products—find a source, quote a price, arrange for delivery. "A call went out to our sourcing team in China to buy and transport to the U.S. as much PPE [personal protective equipment] as they could get their hands on," Patrick recalled. "We were able to airlift a couple million purchased masks, but we quickly realized it wasn't nearly enough."

As the sourcing team frantically worked to meet urgent demand, they pivoted. They started investigating the production bottlenecks that inhibited mask production—including limited capacity to produce the "melt-blown cloth" required for medical masks.

"To produce this material," Patrick explained, "you have to shoot melted polypropylene pellets through a steel tool and die onto a thin film. Mask factories were at their limit. They needed more specialized tooling to increase production."

In what may have felt like a last-ditch effort to meet demand, the sourcing team put the mask industry vendors in touch with Tang Industries' automobile tool and die plant in China, which produces tooling for original equipment manufacturers, to see if they could make the kind of tooling that the mask manufacturers needed. It proved to be a fortuitous connection: Tang Industries *did* have the ability to make the tooling needed for the mask-making machines. But the engineers at Tang went even further—they decided to jury-rig a machine to make the masks themselves.

"The team traded some tooling in exchange for a cast-off husk of an ancient mask machine," Patrick recalled. "The old machine, along with a bunch of cast-off parts and another bunch of new parts which the engineers milled themselves, became the 'Frankenstein' prototype for a mask-producing machine. When their masks were tested at labs in the U.S. and demonstrated that they met regulatory standards, the machine got put into service ASAP to address the pressing shortages in the U.S. So far, we have been able to self-produce two million masks for the U.S. out of the 12–13 million masks that we have shipped to the U.S. thus far, all of which we have either donated or sold at cost," Patrick reported.

Facing constraints, Tang Industries had turned a sourcing problem into an opportunity to serve community needs by creatively using materials at hand.

As Patrick's colleagues did at Tang Industries, anyone working on a problem can explore what happens when you impose constraints. Many questions can prompt your rethinking. Ask yourself: What if I don't have the materials typically needed for production? What if I chose to focus on a very specific target group? What if I limited the timeframe for action? What if I wanted to go for a first small win? What would be a limited experiment that I could try? What could I do if I took away my executive champion, staffing resources, or one stakeholder group? Then work with colleagues to imagine possibilities given these limitations.

▶ LOOK FOR THE OPPORTUNITY WITHIN THE PROBLEM

Another counterintuitive suggestion for problem reframing is to look for a silver lining. Try to find the opportunity embedded in the problem.

This approach is centuries old. Marcus Aurelius, the Roman emperor, wrote that "the impediment to action becomes the action. What stands in the way becomes the way."

Take, for example, the problem of food waste. In the U.S. it is the single largest contributor to the nation's landfills. Eric Myers, director of organics recycling at Waste Management, has been working to address the problem for decades.

"To get a visual of just how big a problem it is," Eric suggested, "simply imagine taking a photo of every food item that you throw away in any given week—from banana peels to that half-eaten Caesar salad." Most of us would be amazed by the quantity of food we personally send to landfills each week. Then imagine that volume on a national scale. In the U.S. alone, we waste over 60 million tons of food annually.[2]

Eric's approach has been to find gold in the midst of orange peels and meat scraps. Under his watch, the company focused on how to create value from wasted food. They tested the feasibility of turning food scraps into green energy, like vehicle fuel and compressed natural gas. Following the success of this new approach, the company has built organic-waste-to-energy recycling projects to date in New York, Boston, and Los Angeles, and it has plans for additional facilities throughout North America.

Also, along the way, Eric, with two other colleagues, was awarded a patent for a new approach for processing sewage that eliminates chemical compounds, including plastics, in the sludge and produces a product that is safe to use.

First Mover Fellows find that lurking somewhere inside each complicated problem is an opportunity waiting to be discovered. When you are facing a problem, ask yourself how you can describe this problem as an opportunity. Try imagining how you can look at the challenges you are facing as a pathway to growth and insight.

▶ TRY AN IDENTIFY MAKEOVER

If you, like me, can't resist before-and-after stories in fashion and home decor magazines, you will want to try the *identify makeover* problem-reframing technique. With this approach, you shift how people see themselves in relation to the problem. With that shift, they look at the problem through a different lens.

One of our Fellows used this approach in engaging with colleagues on a long-standing problem within their company and the scientific community more generally: the lack of gender diversity in decision-making and leadership. Women and men are hired at the same rate, but as they move into middle and executive management, the proportion of women drops dramatically.

The Fellow had worked with colleagues across the company to develop recommendations for increasing diversity, but she knew that not everyone shared her sense of urgency about the problem.

To gain support, she developed a presentation that focused on the recommendations that had emerged from collective conversations within the company. However, she didn't begin by sharing the recommendations. Rather, the first slide of her PowerPoint simply read: "Imagine a girl."

The second slide was a photo of a smiling 13-year-old girl in her soccer gear on a playing field, the Fellow's niece. Across the photo she had written, "This is Sofia."

To her colleagues, the Fellow said, "Think of a young teenage girl in your life—a daughter, a niece, a friend—and project forward 20 years. What are your aspirations for this girl when she grows up?"

She continued by pointing out, based on 2011 U.S. Commerce data, that women held only one-quarter of STEM jobs. Although women earned 60 percent of bachelor's and master's degrees, they held less than 15 percent of executive positions; and their incomes fell short of men's, especially after the age of 35. According to the World Economic Forum, she explained, if that trajectory continued, it would take 118 years to close the economic gap.

By inviting her audience to keep a particular girl in mind and imagine what the professional options could be for this girl 20 years hence, she helped people consider the lack of diversity not as a problem of statistics, but rather as a problem that had long-term implications for someone they cared deeply about.

This approach to helping others think differently about a problem reminds us that the mindset we bring to a specific problem affects the way we see it. Shifting our own mindset and helping others do the same can produce meaningful insights. Questions to ask yourself when you are using the identify makeover technique include: What assumptions are you making about the perspectives of the people involved in the problem? How do people currently involved in the problem describe themselves? How do they approach the problem? If you saw the people involved in the problem as part of the solution to the problem, how would your narrative about them change?

▶ TAKE A STRENGTHS-BASED APPROACH

When we are in problem-solving mode, we understandably focus on what is wrong and how to fix it. However, a powerful strategy for reframing problems is to do a strengths-based analysis rather than to focus on deficiencies. With this approach, you essentially ask, what is going right?

In doing so, you can call on the work of scholars and practitioners who have developed an approach to organizational change called Appreciative Inquiry (AI). Appreciative Inquiry starts with a process of discovery about what is working well and uses those insights to open new paths.[3]

The work by Erin Fitzgerald when she was at the Innovation Center for U.S. Dairy is illustrative.

Early in her career working with dairy farmers across the U.S., Erin realized the need for greater focus on addressing sustainability challenges such as methane gas production, water usage, and waste management. She knew that hammering farmers with gloomy statistics about the environmental impacts of their industry was not a productive way to engage them. Instead, she initiated a broad discovery process. The Innovation Center invited the entire dairy value chain, including dairy farmer families, to talk about sustainability initiatives they had already built into their farming practices. Relying on an Appreciative Inquiry approach, she invited participants to tell stories about what happened when they were working at their best.

These stories reaffirmed the inherent values held by farmers and the entire dairy value chain—such as land and water stewardship and the role they play in feeding the country. And the stories helped them collectively develop a vision for the future. The examples of positive change illuminated what is possible. The Innovation Center used these stories as a foundation for creating a road map for the industry to reduce greenhouse gas emissions by 25 percent by 2020. Innovations ranged from using LED lighting to developing anaerobic digesters, which convert methane-producing manure into renewable natural gas and compost.

Fast-forward to today: The environmental impact of producing a gallon of milk shrank significantly, requiring 30 percent less water and 21 percent less land and making a 19 percent smaller carbon footprint than it did in 2007, when the 2020 goal baseline was set. The industry came together to set a new goal for 2050 to achieve greenhouse gas neutrality, improve water quality, and optimize water use. The industry continues to be a leader in agriculture, fostering collaboration and implementing supply chain strategies from farm to fork, all aimed at achieving sector-wide goals.

Erin resisted the pull of trying to solve the sustainability problem in dairy farming by going straight to critical analysis. This process can produce meaningful insights, but it isn't the only recipe for breakthrough thinking—and it may drive people away from the problem rather than invite them into the solution space. Instead, she invited the community to focus on positive examples of change already in the works.

To use this problem-reframing approach, begin by asking what is already working well. What is best in class about the way you are working? Invite stories about times when the work that you and your colleagues or partners did together felt most impactful, and then explore what conditions enabled these outcomes. Imagine possible futures from that foundation.

▶ TRAVEL IN TIME

Problems are far from static. They may not have existed a few years prior and may not exist a few years from now. Over time they may morph in unpredictable ways. Therefore, another fruitful way to reframe a problem is to look forward and back in time. Consider how the problem you are concerned with might have been defined 10 years ago—or how it may be viewed 10 years hence.

The technology world provides stark examples of how quickly time flies and how much can change in the interim. TikTok now has a billion users around the world, but it didn't even exist until 2016. BookTok, a subcommunity of TikTok formed in 2020, has become so popular that it is driving book sales, putting older books on the top of the bestseller lists, and launching the careers of popular new authors. The first-generation iPhone was introduced in 2007. Today Apple generates over $130 billion annually in revenues from this product. Ten years ago, in 2013, Amazon didn't show up on the Fortune 50 list. In 2023 it is number two.

We certainly don't have to look solely to technology to realize that time changes everything. When the COVID-19 pandemic took hold around the world, our lives changed in countless, unexpected ways almost overnight.

Corporate social intrapreneurs often find that time travel can be a very effective tool for reframing a problem—especially because business decision-making is often singularly focused on costs and benefits in the short term. Reframing a problem with an eye on the future opens new perspectives.

In 2014, one of our Fellows was working in a global company that had won a large five-year contract for work on a project in Brazil. She was responsible for global training and development in the company's production division and had to make sure the company had staff trained and ready to meet the contract obligations.

"The established response to staffing for such a big contract was to bring in expats immediately to get the job done," she explained. She questioned whether that was the right approach and whether they were solving the right problem.

"Rather than focus on this short-term need, I saw that this staffing challenge was a multiyear problem and required a solution that would be appropriate for the long term. Yes, we had the resources now to rely on expat talent, but what about a year from now? We work in a cyclical industry. In another time, we might not have this luxury. I believed we had to prepare for those changes with our operations now.

"I was also aware that the company had made a commitment to create economic value in the communities where we work. But sometimes that commitment took a back seat when a customer wanted an immediate fix."

So she reframed the challenge and asked: How can we look beyond meeting an immediate need and develop a staffing plan that will work over the long term for this contract and others to come?

Pushback came from country managers who wanted to show profitability on the project right away. They also expressed concern about the quality of work they might get from a newly trained team.

"I made the case that training is not a cost," she said. "It's an investment for the long term. And to address their concerns about training, I stressed the importance of trusting the strict guidelines and procedures that we had established for all technical jobs. All employees were trained to perform at a very high standard that is consistent for jobs anywhere in the world."

Her persistence helped colleagues rethink how to staff these contracts. Now, as a result of her prodding, staffing locally at the company is standard practice, including at the management level.

She and other First Movers have found that looking out over time can be a critical way to rethink today's problems. These are some questions that can prompt time-travel thinking: How would colleagues in your company 10 years ago have looked at the situation? How can that backward look help you imagine how the problem might morph over the next 10 years? How has your own perspective on the problem changed over time? How would you and your colleagues see the problem if you believed that the future success of your company depended on getting the framing right?

▶ LEAN INTO YOUR PROBLEM-REFRAMING EXPERTISE

Problem reframing is not an esoteric practice. We do it all the time. We do it when we see a child's misbehavior as a teachable moment rather than an occasion to punish. We do it when we are delayed at an airport, and we use the time as a chance to catch up on reading rather than directing anger toward the airline. We do it when we shift from believing we are so busy that we hardly have time to think, to asking what we could learn if we simply set aside 15 minutes twice a week for reflection. We do it when we commit to listening with an open mind to someone else's point of view on a controversial topic.

However, although we reframe often in our personal lives, we too rarely see problem reframing as a management and innovation skill. Because we are programmed to be problem solvers, we push quickly to get to the answer and spend too little time making sure we have defined the problem correctly. With First Movers, we have found that taking time to practice problem reframing before searching for a solution can make us better problem solvers, not slower ones.

Essential Tools for Changemakers

A map does not just chart, it unlocks and formulates meaning; it forms bridges between here and there, between disparate ideas that we did not know were previously connected.

—REIF LARSON, *THE SELECTED WORKS OF T. S. SPIVET*

CHAPTER 4

Map a Path for Achieving Change

In the initial seminar for our First Movers, we hand each Fellow a blank sheet of paper and a marker and ask them to map the established processes within their company for bringing innovative ideas to life. They get to work, and 15 minutes later, the Fellows' drawings are taped to the walls of the seminar room. The sheets are covered by rectangles and circles, dotted and solid lines, arrows and other process representations—some straightforward, others meandering. Each drawing depicts the "official" change process within their companies.

A partner from IDEO who serves on the Fellowship facilitation team and helps Fellows visualize pathways for achieving change in their companies then reminds the group that while it is critical to understand these established practices, they are rarely useful for getting acceptance for the game-changing ideas championed by corporate social intrapreneurs.

When you are blazing into the white space, there is no GPS to show you the route forward. You need to create your own maps for change.

Diana Simmons's experience at Clif Bar some years ago is a case in point. Diana was responsible for product commercialization and process improvement. The company had publicly committed to using sustainably certified cocoa in all its products—and complete the transition in nine months. She was given responsibility for turning that pledge into practice.

This assignment could be viewed as a corporate intrapreneur's dream—to receive the go-ahead on a project that could deliver business and societal value. Yet she faced the same challenge that all intrapreneurs encounter: the innovation systems already in place were inadequate for meeting this bold commitment. The goalpost was set, but she and her team had to make their way across the field, and there was plenty of interference.

"Even though the company was already using ingredients grown without pesticides and fertilizers whenever possible," Diana explained, "switching to sustainably certified cocoa set a higher bar. It required addressing not only the environmental aspects of our product production, but the economic and social impacts as well. We had to put more focus on human rights and the livelihoods of farmers within our supply chain. The goal was laudable, but the path to achieve it was anything but clear. And the challenges were complex.

"There I was," she recalled, "trying with a large cross-functional team to change our 22-year-old flagship product with the company's existing processes, relationships, and suppliers of all these ingredients. It felt complicated and chaotic, but I had to figure out how to move forward—and fast!"

She and her team took stock of the hurdles they faced, starting with establishing the partnership they needed to achieve the certification they sought. Clif Bar had chosen to work with Rainforest Alliance, which has strict standards for supporting farmers and their communities and the environment. Diana's team had to develop that partnership, understand their standards, and have strategies to meet them.

Her team also faced a product challenge. Clif Bar's many chocolate products contained diverse cocoa ingredients, which were individually sourced. Each had to be studied and changed if necessary, and the product recipes had to be altered in many cases. Of course, to ensure continued customer demand, the product had to taste the same as before.

Further, to achieve certification, the company had to establish a traceable chain of custody for all ingredients—from crops to final bar. Finally, each product required new packaging to showcase the certification. Making all the changes required the involvement of nearly one-third of Clif Bar employees.

Meanwhile, the clock was ticking.

"To keep moving forward," Diana said, "we created a trail map. We identified the milestones, the steps, and the activities that had to be taken to get the job done. But this was not just a typical linear action plan or project timeline. We articulated a topography with all the unanswered questions and potential roadblocks and the assumptions on which the plan was based. Then we could craft the trail through the terrain to get to our summit. When the team hit one of those roadblocks, we would go back to the map and see how we could take another route to the summit. The map allowed us to adapt quickly; it helped us identify and then debate the consequences of making changes to the plan."

It worked. Today 100 percent of cocoa ingredients are organic or sourced from Rainforest Alliance Certified farms.[1]

Charting Your Path

If you were looking at a blank piece of paper and asked to visualize the journey you could take to move from idea to implementation, what route would you take? What guideposts would there be? Who would help you move along the path? Here are some suggestions based on the experiences of our Fellows.

▶ **USE MISSION STATEMENTS AS A BEACON**

Corporate mission statements can be surprisingly useful in making the case for change. Often lofty, these statements frequently reflect a company's social purpose. As you map your path to getting buy-in for change, you may be able to use your company's mission statement as a beacon for others to follow, as Rahul Raj did at Walmart.com, the retail giant's online store.

When Rahul Raj was hired to be director of sustainability and merchandising innovation, the company was early in its sustainability journey. Few executives yet understood what sustainable practices could mean for the company's bottom line.

Rahul, a marketing expert who has long been committed to social and environmental action, was brought in to promote sustainable e-commerce practices, particularly in product packaging. Rahul was in completely new territory, but he eagerly took on the assignment and, in fact, quickly sought wider scope for his efforts.

Rahul was a newcomer to Walmart, but he understood immediately that whatever he proposed had to be related to the core of the business. He did plenty of research to get a deeper understanding of that core, and one thing became very clear. Since Sam Walton founded the company in 1962, Walmart's mission had been unwavering: to help customers save money so they can live better.

The light bulb went on for Rahul. "My job," he realized, "was not to sell sustainability to Walmart. Rather, I had to help Walmart see that there was a ton of money to be made by engaging in a sustainable way. I had to demonstrate that what had previously been considered mutually exclusive—making money and being sustainable—was actually mutually reinforcing. Most importantly, whatever we did needed to help customers save money so they can live better."

As Rahul explained, "I had to figure out what business problem I could help to solve using that framework. So I got time on the calendars of eight executives and asked them what was keeping them up at night. In the process I learned that Walmart's liberal return policy represented a multibillion-dollar expense. I knew that if I could figure out a way to turn this waste stream into a revenue opportunity, I might have a promising idea on my hands.

"There could be a way to strengthen the company's mission and deliver more value for customers," he realized, "if we could reburnish high-value customer returns (like Apple products) to make desirable brands more accessible to customers. We could sell these products on Walmart.com and compete effectively on price against our competitors."

The idea seemed compelling, but he faced pushback from colleagues. They saw the plan as risky. Nobody wanted to jeopardize their job or reputation for an untested idea. Also, as Rahul recalled, "many felt that we were playing a zero-sum game. They believed that if you advanced a social aim—like keeping products from the landfill and offering customers refurbished goods—you would compromise your economic objectives, instead of believing that it's possible to do both. They were also worried that offering refurbished goods at a lower price would

cannibalize sales of other merchandise, and revenue would fall."

Despite skepticism, Rahul got the go-ahead to set up a pilot to test his idea—in part by leaning into the company's mission to help customers save money so they can live better. As a result of offering refurbished electronics, overall sales actually went up and revenues increased. Customers were interested in buying premium brands at value prices and could use the savings to purchase other necessities.

As refurbishing centers were being rolled out across the U.S., Rahul then set out to make the case for an electronics take-back program. The idea was that customers could bring in used electronics and receive market value for the product in the form of a Walmart gift card.

"I was able to show that by encouraging customers to bring back used electronics and giving them fair market value for these items, we were increasing customers' purchasing power in the store—and helping them get rid of stuff they were no longer using. We were also helping to destigmatize refurbished items, by providing the assurance of a warranty, and ensuring that they were accessible to people. If they were spending less money on phones or tablets and getting value from electronics they recycled, they had more money to help their family do other things, like saving for education or buying an extra carton of milk." It was exactly the kind of deal that Sam Walton would have liked.

Walmart was also an early leader in demonstrating the circular economy in action.

Rahul has moved on from Walmart.com, but the take-back program is now well established, and the refurbishment program has generated billions in new revenue. Walmart has even launched a Gadgets to Gift Cards service online.[2] You can get an appraisal for the gadget you wish to recycle, ship it to CExchange, and receive a gift card once the item has been received and evaluated.

▶ POSITION CORPORATE LEGENDS AS ON-RAMPS

I was introduced to the idea of corporate *myths* by Fred Dust, a former partner at IDEO and early member of the First Movers design team.

Myths, as Fred called them, are the stories, the sagas, the corporate legends, that embody the assumptions that drive behavior in organizations.

All organizations have them. (Families have them too, by the way. As a parent—and now grandparent—since hearing Fred talk about myths, I have thought a great deal about the pervasive stories in my own family and how they enable or inhibit our outlooks and actions.)

Whether rooted in fact or fiction, corporate myths are powerful magnetic fields on a corporate compass. Often they influence without being explicitly named or referenced.

Think of your own corporate culture. Do any of these assertions sound familiar? "We promote on merit." "We embrace failure." "We are anti-bureaucratic." "Corporate managers are obligated by law to make decisions that maximize shareholder value." "Radical candor is essential for strong corporate culture."

As an intrapreneur, you need to recognize and name these corporate legends and position them on your map. Only when you are clear about what they are can you be intentional about using them as an on-ramp to support your efforts or finding effective ways to maneuver around them.

Suzanne Howard, a First Mover herself and member of the facilitation team during her time as a partner at IDEO, refers to these kinds of corporate stories as "sacred cows." She knows firsthand the importance of being aware of these stories, the "truths" that underpin decision-making.

When Suzanne was working as an intrapreneur within IDEO, the "truth" she had to confront was the widely shared belief that innovation had to be taught in person. She challenged that conviction and over several years led the creation of IDEO U, an online platform for learning about innovation and design thinking that now reaches thousands of eager learners around the world and produces revenues for IDEO.

Legends about corporate founders are a particularly useful example of stories that resonate within a company. Think of Steve Jobs at Apple. Thomas Edison at General Electric. Henry Ford at Ford Motor Company. Years after a company's founding, many decisions continue to be based on what employees assume their founders would do in the present circumstance.

Corporate intrapreneurs can often take advantage of companies' origin stories by using the principles embedded in them to bolster the case

MAP

for a social innovation—as Paul Ellingstad did when he was director of human progress initiatives at Hewlett Packard.

Paul's job was to implement a creating shared value (CSV) model at scale into the company's culture and operating model. *Creating shared value* refers to "the practice of creating economic value in a way that also creates value for society by addressing its needs and challenges," as described by Michael Porter and Mark Kramer in a 2011 article in the *Harvard Business Review*. In this model, the social value created does not come as a cost to the company. As Porter and Kramer explained, "By better connecting companies' success with societal improvement, it opens up many ways to serve new needs, gain efficiency, create differentiation, and expand markets."[3]

To create shared value at HP, Paul recalled, "I focused on opportunities in global health and sought to understand what unique value HP could bring into this complex ecosystem."

Given the extreme technology lag in health systems in low- and middle-income countries, Paul believed HP could create significant business and social value if it worked with local governments and combined its deep expertise in technology with the health expertise offered by organizations like the Clinton Health Access Initiative (CHAI) and Partners in Health.

"CSV called for a completely different business model," Paul explained. "In the past, any investments HP had made in these countries had been financed with philanthropic dollars and foreign aid. The expenditures weren't treated as business development opportunities. They were seen as a cost. Creating shared value provided a framework for linking financial and social objectives that leveraged corporate responsibility budgets in new ways and prioritized expenditures that aligned with commercial objectives."

Despite the appeal of the new model, HP was facing financial challenges at the time, and many colleagues argued that the company could ill afford to expend resources on risky new bets. Paul invoked the company's famous founding story to help him make the case.

In the late 1930s, even before Bill Hewlett and David Packard had a clear vision for a product line, these two young electrical engineers from

Stanford University set out the principles that would serve as a foundation for the company they hoped to start. These principles, summarized in a famous speech that David Packard made to HP managers in 1960, came to be known as the HP Way.

In that speech, Packard talked about why a company exists. He said that many people assume that it is simply to make money. While acknowledging that making money is important, he insisted that it is not the real reason for being. Rather, he believed, people get together to create companies "so they are able to accomplish something collectively which they could not accomplish separately. They are able to do something worthwhile—they make a contribution to society."[4] That speech became lore at the company.

Decades later, Paul would often reference the speech to help make his case for a new approach for doing business. With this boost from the founders' vision, Paul ultimately gained support from colleagues for shared value projects. HP then began by working in partnership with the health ministry in Kenya, CHAI, and Strathmore University in Nairobi to achieve groundbreaking digital transformation of key health services.

These partners initially focused on HIV testing procedures for infants, which dramatically sped up the turnaround time for getting results and beginning treatment for infected infants. This work catalyzed improvements made through digitalization across the public health services. Beyond the transformational, often lifesaving impact, there was a clear business benefit for HP as well. The company established its bona fides as a global health solutions provider, built credibility with the governments of Kenya and other nations, and opened doors to other business opportunities.[5]

▶ ENLIST INFLUENCERS AS TRAVEL GUIDES

The established processes for change in companies generally point to the individuals who have explicit authority to give ideas a green light. You need access to some senior vice president, for example, to get traction, because they control the budget or allocation of staff time. But some individuals who don't show up on the innovation process org chart often have considerable unofficial influence. Your job is to find them and get them engaged.

As Suzanne Howard advised, "Look for the one who has the secret keys." They are the trendsetters, the next-in-line, the ones who have the ear of the official decision maker.

As you seek out these individuals, do not bypass colleagues who express skepticism about your ideas. "Ask yourself, who are you most scared to talk to?" Suzanne suggested. Skeptics (not cynics) can prove to be the most useful partners. Their questions can help you see critical factors that you may have missed. If you pay attention to what they have to say and don't assume they are simply dismissing your ideas, you may find that they offer fresh ways of looking at the opportunity or minimizing possible risks. If you can get the skeptics on board, not only will your idea be more robust because of their input, but they may become your biggest champions. In Suzanne's case, the influential skeptic she approached when she was just beginning to imagine how to offer training online became one of her most important thought partners in building IDEO U.

As they think about who might serve as a travel guide, some Fellows create stakeholder maps, which provide a visual representation of all the people who can influence decisions about their projects. This activity prompts them to take a more expansive view on who needs to be involved to improve the chances of generating energy around an idea. With this map in hand, they build an outreach plan and start to schedule exploratory conversations with these individuals.

▶ TAKE ADVANTAGE OF TAILWINDS

"You have to make the business case" is the refrain heard constantly by all corporate social intrapreneurs. For years, that admonition meant that to get support to move forward with a social innovation, you had to "prove" that the project would deliver growth or profits. In essence, it had to help a company maximize its value to shareholders—and lead to a higher stock price, preferably in the short term.

Today, employees, investors, customers, and community members are expecting much more from companies than delivering value for shareholders. These changes in public sentiment have created powerful tailwinds for intrapreneurs.

Some believe the sea change occurred on August 19, 2019, when the Business Roundtable (BRT), an association of nearly 200 CEOs from some of the largest companies in the U.S., released a statement that reverberated in the business press around the world. The headline read, "Business Roundtable Redefines the Purpose of a Corporation to Promote 'An Economy That Serves All Americans.'"[6] Previously, the BRT definition of corporate purpose rested on the notion that companies had to put shareholders above all others. Now these CEOs were saying it was critical to lead their companies for the benefit of all their stakeholders—which they named as customers, employees, suppliers, communities, and shareholders. (Left unmentioned, by the way, was any commitment to the health of the planet.)

In fact, this change had been coming for some time. Many advocates, like my colleagues at the Aspen Institute Business & Society Program, forward-looking business leaders and academics, and other groups, had argued for overthrowing shareholder primacy for two decades. Also, even before the BRT released its statement, mainstream investors, whose opinion has significant influence within executive suites and boardrooms, were coming around to the realization that corporate value over the long term would be undermined if companies ignored environmental and social risks and would be enhanced if companies took advantage of opportunities presented by social and environmental trends.

An investor in the forefront of this movement is Thomas Kamei, a First Mover Fellow and executive director and investor at Counterpoint Global at Morgan Stanley Investment Management. His investment track record earned him the designation in 2018 as one of *Forbes'* 30 Under 30: Finance.

Many who know Thomas's exceptional work in the investment arena might be surprised to learn that he got his undergraduate degree in architecture and has a keen interest in art and design. But his passion for understanding the financial markets is long-standing. At the prodding of his mother, an investment analyst, Thomas attended his first Berkshire Hathaway annual meeting when he was six years old and has been to every meeting since then. During the meeting in 2000, when Thomas was only 10, he boldly asked Warren Buffett what the impact of the internet would be on his investments.

Thomas continues to ask bold questions. "Every day I get into the office," he told me, "I have one job. I'm fiduciarily bound to try to create alpha." In other words, he must constantly strive to generate excess returns for his clients—without incurring additional risks. Now leading sustainability research at Counterpoint Global, Thomas believes deeply that alpha can be found by understanding the way companies manage environmental and social risks and opportunities.

He is helping other Fellows think more strategically about how to reframe intended social and environmental outcomes into financial terms. His insights are critical for all innovators who need to "make the business case."

Thomas points out that if you can demonstrate that your idea will unlock new markets, you can climb on the growth bandwagon. If your idea can lead to operational efficiencies (such as attracting purpose-driven talent or retaining workers or reducing energy costs), you can show that it will boost profitability.

If you can frame your idea as helping your company reduce the risks associated with increased pressure from regulators and others for expanded disclosure on environmental, social, and governance (ESG) factors, you can make a compelling financial case.

Finally, if your idea creates a competitive advantage by helping you to get ahead of others in your industry on social and environmental trends, you can position the opportunity as "expanding the moat," a reference to the wide, water-filled ditches that protected castles from attackers.

Effective social intrapreneurs take full advantage of these tailwinds.

For years, we have asked First Movers what enabled them to succeed in achieving changes—big and small. Among the characteristics they often cite is their organizational savvy.

Mapping a change process allows you to tap into your savvy, slow down, and visualize the journey from concept to reality.

I alone cannot change the world,
but I can cast a stone across the waters
to create many ripples.

—MOTHER TERESA

CHAPTER 5

Seek Small Wins to Build Momentum for Big Change

D espite the determination of corporate social intrapreneurs to use the platform of business to solve complex social and environmental challenges, it is easy to get overwhelmed by the scope of the change needed to address them. The problems are simply too big.

One way they move forward is to go for the small wins and deliberately build momentum from there.

Karl Weick, an organizational theorist, helps us to understand the importance of shifting from a focus on massive, seemingly intractable social problems toward a limited definition of what needs to be solved. That reframe can then empower us to act.

In his article "Small Wins: Redefining the Scale of Social Problems," Weick writes, "People often define social problems in ways that overwhelm their ability to do anything about them." Doing so raises our anxiety, and in that mental state we feel powerless to act.[1]

To lower emotion around the problem, Weick argues, we should look for a way to achieve a strategic small win, which he describes as "a concrete, complete, implemented outcome of moderate importance." A small win can have a cascading effect. It can make the possibilities for subsequent wins more visible.

Chip Heath and Dan Heath offer similar advice. In *Switch: How to Change Things When Change Is Hard*, they point out that "big problems are rarely solved with commensurately big solutions. Instead they are most often solved by a sequence of small solutions, sometimes over weeks, sometimes over decades."[2] And they show readers how to "shrink the change" to achieve "milestones within reach."[3]

Understandably, some Fellows are troubled by the notion of small wins to address social and environmental problems they see as urgent and existential threats to our collective well-being.

As one Fellow said in a recent seminar, "Small wins may have been good for a time we are no longer in, but in the face of entrenched racism, a small win seems cheap." Likewise, as the planet heats up, and droughts, floods, and fires take a devastating toll, some believe that revolution rather than reform may be the only way to make a lasting difference.

We acknowledge these concerns and understand reluctance to embrace change that seems incremental. That is why we emphasize that for small wins to really help us make progress in addressing a complex problem, they must be strategic tools for change rather than one-off victories.

Small wins are controllable and constrained, requiring a limited amount of time, effort, skill, and expense. But they can lead to results that reverberate. "Once a small win has been accomplished," Weick suggests, "forces are set in motion that favor another small win. When a solution is put in place, the next solvable problem often becomes more visible. This occurs because new allies bring new solutions with them and old opponents change their habits. Additional resources also flow toward winners, which means that slightly larger wins can be attempted."[4]

Achieving this cascading effect depends on the ability of people to tell the story of the results in ways that inform and engage others. It also requires that they stay alert to other, related small wins and begin to see patterns that signal progress. Weick notes that these achievements rarely follow a linear pattern. Savvy corporate social intrapreneurs are able to construct a "retrospective summary" of related wins rather than relying on a grand strategy for progress. "Much of the artfulness in working with small wins lies in identifying, gathering, and labeling several small changes that are present but unnoticed," Weick writes.[5]

In the stories that follow, you'll see how First Movers make progress on wicked problems by going for one small, strategic win at a time.

Expanding Job Opportunities

In the U.S. and elsewhere, economic mobility is extremely limited for a significant percentage of the population, and the wealth gap is growing. One of the many reasons is that access to job opportunities is inequitably distributed. Nontraditional job seekers without degrees, an employment track record, or connections face multiple challenges in the job market.

Two Fellows are determined to help these people get to work, and they are leading innovative efforts at their companies to create digital platforms that crack open pathways to employment for nontraditional workers.

Abigail Carlton is vice president of social impact at Indeed, an online job site that gets more than 350 million unique visitors every month. Abigail believes that résumés that highlight a job seeker's educational background and job history are poor indicators of a person's actual job skills.

So she has worked with tech colleagues to build a skills-based screening platform, called Indeed Assessments, which allows these job seekers to showcase their qualifications—not their degrees and previous titles. Prospective employers can request that candidates complete these assessments, or job seekers can opt to do the assessments on their own and post their results online. The Indeed website also provides helpful tips for job seekers taking these tests. It acknowledges that taking assessment tests can be stressful, so it advises candidates to browse through test options and get acclimated to the testing process by taking some assessments that are not directly relevant to the jobs they are seeking. Those practice runs will help them understand the format of these tests, the way questions are posed, and how to manage the timing.

Like Abigail, Hari Srinivasan, vice president of product at LinkedIn, believes that a "skills first" rather than "credentials first" approach is a critical way to give more people access to gainful employment. So his team is building additional functionality into the LinkedIn platform. They are bringing skills to the forefront of their LinkedIn Recruiter product so that employers will more easily be able to find candidates that match their skills requirements. Hari's team is also offering the LinkedIn

Learning Hub, where job seekers can earn certificates for completing courses on a wide range of topics. Also, LinkedIn members are now able to add skills to their profiles. This feature appears to be hugely popular. Nearly 300 million skills were added by members in 2021.

These digital offerings won't fully solve the challenge of achieving greater economic mobility for many who are not thriving in the current system, but they do provide an on-ramp that is taking millions of workers in the right direction. Both Indeed and LinkedIn are able to track in real time the success of various platform adaptations. These metrics can then lead to further experimentation.

Humanizing Corporate Digital Transformations

Companies spend nearly $2 trillion a year on digital transformation, and that amount is projected to grow by another $1.8 trillion by 2026.[6] Nevertheless, roughly 70 percent of these transformations fail.[7]

Hao Dinh, vice president of technology at EnPro, an industrial technology company, has had a front-row seat at digital transformation initiatives at several multinational corporations over the years and believes these failures often happen because companies don't think carefully enough about the people affected by the changes. His personal mission is to enable everyone to be digital and to help companies engage employees in the change process, rather than simply impose change upon them.

"Executives focus on the technology," Hao told me, "which distracts them from considering the toll these changes take on employees and the training and education needed to effect a successful transformation."

Aiming for strategic, small wins, Hao works within companies to run pilots with workers to help them become more comfortable with technology and achieve modest changes that lay a foundation for larger transformation initiatives. And he keeps management apprised of progress.

For example, Hao recalled a story about factory employees in a company that wanted to digitize data collection and move away from its age-old use of paper.

"One employee was willing to try to build an app for this purpose," Hao said. "We gave him a small amount of money and told him to go ahead. He formed a small team and started to work. The team created a prototype, tested it with users, and kept iterating on the design."

Building this app together gave employees control of the process and a glimpse of the digitized future. The factory-level collaboration changed the tone in the plant. As Hao recounted, "Every time we had a revision of the app, the plant employees were involved and realized that the digitalization transition *is* possible and that the financial savings could be significant. Moreover, they felt fully invested in the effort.

"When employees feel a part of the change," Hao explained, "they are less likely to see themselves as victims of inexorable forces. They take one step in the direction of being part of the solution."

More recently, he worked on a pilot with about 100 equipment maintenance engineers in a factory where management planned to introduce big data and artificial intelligence (AI) tools. These engineers had not worked with these tools and had deep anxiety about what these changes could mean for their jobs.

Hao sought to involve the engineers early in the process so they could appreciate how using these tools would enhance, not eliminate, their work.

Hao and his team developed training sessions to help the engineers understand what big data and AI were about and how they could improve preventive maintenance on machines. They also hoped to show the maintenance engineers how their expertise could complement technology.

The team asked the engineers to identify the biggest headaches they had with their machines and which ones were most problematic. The team took all the data through the AI tools to produce recommendations for processes that would prevent breakdowns. Then, with the engineers, the team studied the recommendations. Only a tiny percentage of the recommendations proved useful.

In the next phase of the pilot, the team worked with the engineers to develop the AI algorithms that would predict when the machines would fail. When the engineers were involved, the predictions turned out to be about 30 percent accurate. In the end, by combining data, AI, and human expertise, they were able to increase the "up time" of the machines, which was highly beneficial for the organization.

These engineers, initially suspicious of efforts to digitize their work, now understood that they played a key role in the digitalization effort and could access these tools to enhance their outcomes. This small win lowered their anxiety about further changes to come.

Hao repeatedly tells this story—and others—to senior executives to illustrate how investing in human capital is critical for achieving the digital transformation they seek. He builds from one small win to the next to make his case and along the way gets corporate buy-in for additional investments in training and testing, to make digital transformation more humane.

Hao is also a realist. He knows that these transformations will certainly lead to the loss of many jobs and will require upskilling for others. So while he pilots programs within companies to demonstrate to employees how they can learn and benefit from these changes, he also works with community resource groups and community colleges to develop training programs to build new skills for those who are displaced and willing and able to be retrained, as well as to develop solid outplacement services for others. He is determined to change the system, one small win at a time.

Linking Climate Action and Environmental Justice

Achieving corporate environmental goals or racial equity goals alone is difficult enough. But companies now realize that to make real progress on either front, they must consider the linkages between the two.

Emily Alati, director of materials innovation at Vans, the action sports footwear and clothing company, is undaunted by the challenge. She has been fascinated by the world of apparel since she was a child. "I started to sew when I was five," she recalled. "I loved it. I even made dresses for my poor cats." She studied fashion design in college but then became more interested in the materials in the clothes than in the design. After getting her master's degree in textile science and process engineering, she joined Timberland, then a family-owned company dedicated to minimizing its environmental footprint.

Vans and Timberland are now part of VF Corporation, one of the largest apparel and footwear companies in the world, with a mission to power movements of sustainable and active lifestyles for the betterment of people and our planet.

Emily has an ambitious long-term goal of integrating climate action and environmental justice in the industry where she has worked for 20 years. She wants to build an eco-accelerator to provide a way for Vans to bring underrepresented groups, mainly women and people of color, into the company's supply chain and to encourage more sustainable farming practices. "The accelerator would fundamentally change the way the company produces and procures its three principal materials—rubber, cotton, and leather," Emily explained. "Over time, it would revolutionize farming and harvesting of these products by moving to a regenerative model of agriculture. It would also alter the face of farming by attracting people of color and women into the profession."

It may sound like an impossible dream, but Emily spends little time thinking about how hard it is to achieve sweeping change in systems. Instead, she is focused on a few farmers and one crop.

In 2021, Emily was running an experimental program to grow industrial hemp and test its use as a sustainable alternative to cotton. But in the wake of the racial reckoning in the U.S. following the murder of George Floyd, she resolved to look at this work through an environmental justice lens. She asked herself, "What if we could ensure that some of the farmers we are working with in this venture are Black?" She contacted a colleague who knows the farming community in North Carolina, and soon they found two Black farmers in North Carolina willing to participate.

Hemp farming, Emily said, has benefits for both farmers and the planet. For starters, hemp grows fast. Also, growing hemp gives farmers an opportunity to rotate crops and provides another revenue stream. Further, growing hemp can contribute to soil health not only because of the rotation but also because hemp plants take toxic particles out of the ground. Moreover, if industrial hemp is grown properly, farmers can generate carbon credits, which they can sell into the market. Each of these attributes gives farmers more reasons to shift from traditional farming methods to regenerative ones.

She hopes the pilot will demonstrate the possibility of linking climate goals and environmental justice and will point toward steps that

VF Corporation can take over 3 to 10 years. If the work is ultimately as successful as she hopes, it will change the entire apparel and footwear industry, a change she acknowledges could take 25 years.

But right now she is building momentum from the achievement of a small win: a successful first season. The two Black farmers have agreed to continue to experiment for another year, and two more Black farmers have committed to participate.

"It was easy to start this pilot with the help of a small number of colleagues," she said. "As work progressed, I shared positive results with others, who then shared the story within their networks." For example, Emily says she has gotten an enthusiastic response from the merchandising team, the group that must figure out which products the hemp will go in, which market segment they will target, and how the product will be marketed.

Emily has also been invited to present early insights from the pilot at VF, the holding company for Vans. Executives are asking how they can get involved. The story of the pilot's early success is prompting them to think about how they could achieve greater racial equity across the company's entire supply chain. "Not only has this enthusiasm allowed us to get funding to support the Vans project," Emily told me, "but we agreed to put together a working group with participants from the company and with experts from the underrepresented groups so that we can learn more about this space and then design a strategy together to move forward."

Meeting the World's Water and Wastewater Needs

The United Nations estimates that water scarcity affects more than two billion people, and climate change is making the problem worse.[8] The funding gap to solve water problems continues to grow. In the U.S. alone, an estimated $250 billion over 30 years will be needed to replace worn drinking water pipes and fixtures to ensure that everyone has access to safe water. And more will be needed for wastewater infrastructures.[9]

Randolf Waters, with a surname befitting his commitment, is dedicated to making a dent in the problem.

Trained as an engineer, he joined Xylem, a leading water technology company, in 2015 after working as a sustainability consultant. He wanted to fully dedicate his time to the world of water and technology, and with Xylem's tagline of "Let's Solve Water," he knew he had found the perfect place.

"Typically," Randolf explained, "municipal water systems fund their operations through tariffs, municipal bonds, and federal funding. But this funding always falls short, and the infrastructure issues worsen over time. I started to wonder if Xylem, and private financiers, could provide new types of financing to accelerate the deployment of advanced technologies that deliver near-term fixes and over the long term reduce the cost of operations, ultimately enabling the utility company to deliver water and wastewater services that are affordable for all."

With that idea in mind, he worked with colleagues across the company, including legal, finance, and product teams, to explore the options. Eventually they settled on a financing structure they could test in the market.

It is a financial model whereby repayment is based on product performance. If the pumps perform as promised, the up-front capital cost is reduced, and the savings are shared between Xylem and the customer.

"Once the stars aligned and we found a customer for this new structure," Randolf reported, "we leaned on our strong customer relationship to get a pilot sorted and create some internal buzz about where to take it next."

By developing this new financing model, they moved one step forward in the long process of helping municipalities cover the costs of meeting their water needs.

Strategies for Creating Small Wins That Can Build Toward Bigger Change

The experiences of these Fellows and others offer lessons for those who have decided to contribute their expertise and take advantage of their platform within business to solve really tough social problems but need a boost to find a way to move forward.

▶ EMBRACE PILOTING AND PROTOTYPING

Since the beginning of the First Movers Fellowship, we have benefited from our collaboration with IDEO, a world-renowned design firm. One of the many ways that IDEO partners have contributed to the Fellowship experience is by helping Fellows become more adept at piloting and prototyping. These processes are a cornerstone of design thinking, an approach to innovation that relies on shared generation of creative ideas and iterative experimentation.

IDEO partners advise Fellows, "Start small. Start now," to answer the fundamental question of "How might we . . . ?" Prototyping and piloting allows you to make an idea tangible by creating a rough representation that people can experience. As Suzanne Howard from IDEO explained, "A prototype is a question embodied." (Courses available on IDEO U, the online university that Suzanne created, make it easy for anyone to learn fundamental principles of piloting and prototyping and put them to use immediately.)

Hao Dinh is an ardent advocate of design thinking and the benefits of piloting. "Too many companies rely on an annual planning process," he said. "Every January they go through strategy planning for the next year and then in March allocate X million dollars to projects. The rest of the year they execute against that plan. These plans are announced, and employees are expected to get on board."

Instead of relying on annual strategic plans, Hao stated, "you need to meet every two weeks, allocate a small amount of funding for a pilot effort, run the experiment, and then check in at the end of the period. At that point you can harvest your learning and move forward or pivot."

Hao's experience also demonstrates another advantage of piloting: it allows you to fly under the corporate radar to get things done. In most large companies, Hao explained, to introduce a major new product, service, or management practice, you need to work through complex, established change processes. Gaining access to those processes typically requires obtaining significant buy-in from senior decision makers. To get a green light, you must demonstrate the potential impact of the innovation at scale. Not only do you have to believe that something will work, but you have to show evidence of its benefits.

In contrast, when you design an experiment that aims for quick learning and possibly leads you to a small win (or loss), you can legitimately justify giving it a try by saying, "It's just a pilot." It gives you leeway to act outside the formal system.

Emily Alati agrees. She knows what it takes at Vans to get a new material into the traditional sourcing and production process. Plans are approved and put in place. Milestone dates are established. "These controls make sense," Emily acknowledged. "This kind of careful planning ensures quality and budget control and mitigates risk. But if you call something a pilot, you signal that the risk is much smaller, and the cost is minimal. So you can avoid these requirements."

▶ PREPARE CAREFULLY AND BE PATIENT

Even when going for a win seems to be a relatively small effort, you cannot count on change happening quickly.

It took Randolf Waters three years of work with multiple colleagues at Xylem to get the innovative financing structure off the ground—much longer than he had anticipated.

"The biggest lesson I've learned," Randolf reflected, "is to be patient. You have to be willing to wait for all of the stars to align, internally and with customers. We did a ton of prep work to develop the idea, engage external experts, socialize the concept, gain buy-in internally, etc., and then it turned into six months of waiting to find the right customer."

Randolf also discovered that delays can have unexpected benefits. They can "provide critical time for the pilot idea to percolate among those involved in the work. It gives people time to get used to the idea and digest it." Also, Randolf said, "letting it linger—and involving many colleagues in the conceptualization and design—allows people who are involved to co-opt the idea and become a driving force."

Abigail, Hari, Hao, Emily, and Randolf show how achieving even small progress against seemingly insurmountable problems can produce energizing results. All are passionate about change and optimistic that it can happen. They are also tenacious and pragmatic. They are in training for the long haul.

At least in Hao's case, he learned the importance of long-haul training outside of work. Professional skateboarding doesn't show up on his impressive professional profile, even though he says it was his favorite job. But being a competitive skateboarder is one of the ways Hao has become comfortable facing big challenges and taking controlled risks. He didn't become a champion skateboarder by starting with 900-degree flips. He learned how to balance first.

▶ CREATE A NARRATIVE THAT LEVERAGES THE WIN

The victory lap after achieving a small win can be sweet, but it must also be short. The next part of the race is to create a narrative that spotlights the meaning and potential of the win. The stories you tell are critical for ensuring that the small win becomes more than an isolated accomplishment.

"You have to tell the story over and over again," Emily advised. As we saw earlier, Emily's storytelling has had a snowball effect within Vans and at the parent company. She has gotten additional funding for her work. Colleagues are indicating that they want to get involved, and they are seeing other possibilities for piloting new approaches. They have created a learning group so that they have diverse perspectives on what is needed and what is possible for them to achieve as they strive for greater integration of environmental justice into their work.

Hao Dinh is also dedicated to creating a narrative around small wins. He has regular meetings with senior executives to report on progress and tells stories about his work with employees on the factory floor. These stories provide opportunities for executives to foresee a different future, offer input on what steps they could take next, and approve the next pilot.

For Randolf, creating a narrative around the pilot was critical for demonstrating that innovative financing could be an important step forward in addressing municipalities' huge infrastructure needs. The narrative was powerful for both customers and the company. For customers, they had a story of how thinking creatively benefited communities in need in a more cost-effective way. For the company, they had a story of how thinking creatively met the customer need, deepened key relationships, and accelerated the sale of the technology solution and an associated maintenance contract.

Many First Movers also find that they have the opportunity to share stories about small wins not only within the company but to a wider audience within their industry and beyond. As word of Emily's work on hemp growing with Black farmers has gotten out, she has repeatedly been asked to speak at conferences on a range of topics—from regenerative agriculture to strategies for finding and working with underrepresented farmers.

Hao Dinh is frequently invited to conferences on manufacturing, digital workplaces, and innovation. In each venue he stays on message: for the digitalization revolution to be successful for companies and employees, companies need to do more to consider the human costs and opportunities associated with these changes. And he shares stories from his own experience about how companies are learning how to navigate these changes, which encourages others to try new approaches.

Randolf Waters has had similar experiences. "That initial pilot was back in 2017," he said, "and sparked a number of C-suite customer conversations and conference invitations both in the world of water and finance. Even to this day, after I've moved roles multiple times, the topic of innovative financing in water is one I still am pulled into every few months."

These speaking opportunities aren't simply a way for Fellows to gain notoriety. They are part of the effort to demonstrate that making headway on large problems by aiming for small wins is possible, and they show others how to start or how to keep going. This collective effort is critical. The problems that First Movers are trying to address require change at the level of the system. One company, no matter how determined and successful, can accomplish only so much.

As Chip Heath and Dan Heath explain, "When you engineer early successes, what you are really doing is engineering hope. Hope is precious to a change effort."[10] Stories that First Movers tell within their companies and beyond spread that hope and ignite a sense of possibility among others, who are then inspired to achieve small wins for big change within their own organizations.

*Storytelling offers the opportunity
to talk with your audience, not at them.*

—LAURA HOLLOWAY, FOUNDER AND CHIEF
OF THE STORYTELLER AGENCY

CHAPTER 6

Tell Stories and Invite Others to Tell Theirs

The first seminar of the inaugural class of First Mover Fellows convened in Aspen, Colorado, in July 2009. To begin, we asked each Fellow to tell a five-minute story of a time when they were working at their best to create value for their company and for society. The design team hoped that launching the program with these stories would set the tone for all that was to come. But we had no idea how the storytelling would play out.

Suzanne Ackerman, then–transformation director at Pick n Pay, a leading supermarket chain in South Africa, volunteered to go first. She stood up and pulled out a crumpled piece of paper. Without prologue, she read a letter of gratitude from Sibusiso Tshabalala.

Tshabalala makes firewood. With Suzanne's help, he had turned his grandfather's woodcutting and charcoal venture into a thriving enterprise. As a result, he no longer had to sell his wares by the side of the road. He had learned how to standardize, package, and distribute his products and had become a major supplier to Pick n Pay. He now had a steady income. His life had been transformed, and his letter was a poignant thank-you to Suzanne for helping him turn his dreams into reality.

When she sat down, the room was quiet. And the facilitation team let out a silent sigh of relief. Suzanne had captured the essence of what First Movers do best. They create opportunities, possibilities, and connections that can lead to changes in business practices and in people's lives. With her story and those that followed on that warm afternoon in Aspen, we knew we had tapped into rich ore.

Suzanne had lots of statistics that she could have shared. She could have told us that her work was helping Pick n Pay comply with South African Black Economic Empowerment mandates. Or she could have wowed us with her track record empowering small, minority business owners to become suppliers to powerful retailers like Pick n Pay. Instead, she told us the story of a single entrepreneur. And in a few words, she communicated something much deeper that captured our attention and encouraged others to do the same.

Over the next couple of hours, other Fellows picked up on her lead as they recounted stories from their own journeys. As the session finished, we all felt a greater connection to each other. Without viewing a single PowerPoint slide, we had a deep sense of what each of these Fellows had accomplished and their commitment to achieving more ahead.

When we designed the seminars for First Mover Fellows, we knew that storytelling was an important skill for change agents, and we incorporated storytelling practice into the design of the seminars for Fellows. However, we have been surprised by the number of Fellows who underscore how much they value the emphasis we place on it.

Ajay Badhwar, an engineer who was at Dow Chemical when he was selected for the Fellowship, put it succinctly: "Coming into the program, I described problems through data and market dynamics; I now rely more on compelling stories to present problems and solutions to get buy-in from senior leadership."

Another Fellow commented that before her exposure to storytelling in the program, she thought stories were more for children than for the workplace. Once she realized their impact in a professional setting, she resolved to make stories a central part of the way she talked about her work, and it has paid off. By leveraging both data and stories, she has achieved project success and enhanced her value to the company.

Storytelling is a practice available to all. However, you must first consciously choose to include it in your skill set. Then you can study what makes a story compelling and find techniques that work for you.

Many of us freeze at the idea of being a storyteller—especially if you, like me, have found yourself in the middle of telling a joke and realized you were heading for a crash landing. For years I had internalized a narrative about myself that I couldn't tell jokes, and, by extension, I couldn't tell stories. But what I know now is that learning how to use and tell stories effectively does not mean you need to become a stand-up comic or professional raconteur. It simply means you need to get better at deciding what you want to say and how to do it so that people will listen and remember your message.

Peter Guber, producer of such legendary films as *Batman*, *The Color Purple*, and *Rain Man*, stresses that the most effective stories rest on four truths: Stories must be true to the teller, to the audience, to the moment, and to the mission.[1]

Suzanne's story addressed all four dimensions of these truths. She spoke about her own truth—a deep commitment to help minority entrepreneurs become part of Pick n Pay's supply chain. The story was true for the audience of corporate changemakers who could appreciate the dual value she was creating—for her company and for society. Her story was right for the moment—as we began a training program together to build capacity to achieve this kind of change. Finally, it was in sync with the mission of the First Movers Fellowship Program as well as with Suzanne's personal purpose.

Pointers for Telling Stories That Get Results

As I have listened to Fellows tell their stories and made a point of studying the art of storytelling, I have learned about what makes some far more memorable and impactful than others. I share these lessons here to help you tell stories that stick.

▶ **TELL STORIES ABOUT PEOPLE**
The work that Suzanne Ackerman has been championing at the company since she was selected for the inaugural class of First Mover Fellows in 2009 is to disrupt Pick n Pay's supply chain. By mentoring small-scale South African farmers and entrepreneurs, many of whom are Black, she

seeks to ensure that they have a chance of becoming reliable suppliers to this retail business and thus having a dependable livelihood.

She has moved this work forward one story at a time. There is the story of Sibusiso Tshabalala and his charcoal business. She also tells the story of Ntombie Nonxuba, founder and director of Rise Uniforms, who has loved to sew since she was eight. With Suzanne's help, she now supplies uniforms to Pick n Pay employees and employs 10 women from squatter camps in her business. And there is the story of Anna Phosa, founder and owner of Dreamland Piggery. With help from Pick n Pay, Phosa has become the most successful female Black commercial pig farmer on the continent of Africa. Starting with four small pigs, she has built a business that now employs 46 people and that reliably supplies pork to Pick n Pay.

These stories have helped Suzanne get buy-in, demonstrate impact, and achieve remarkable results. The Enterprise Supplier and Development Program she started has become an important department of Pick n Pay's business. It provides training and mentorship for more than 100 small Black businesses and farmers. Along the way, this work has also helped Pick n Pay move up in its ranking on the Black Economic Empowerment score, as certified by the government.

Every corporate social intrapreneur is trying to make the world a better place *for people*. There is a lot of talk these days about companies shifting from profit maximizing for shareholders to practicing something called *stakeholder capitalism*. With that move, companies are pledging to serve multiple groups—including customers, employees, community members, all those affected by climate change, *and* shareholders. It is a laudable intent, but there is a danger when we talk about serving "stakeholders." It is not clear who is really being impacted.

Similarly, when corporate changemakers talk about complicated issues they want to tackle, like climate change, diversity and inclusion, human rights, economic inequity, and so many others, the underlying problems can feel abstract and remote to listeners. Talking about people affected by these problems is more likely to get listeners interested and engaged.

When you are making the case for a new product, service, or management practice, you are much more likely to get colleagues on board if you can first get them to see what the impact would be on people—or even one person.

For example, suppose you are recommending a change in compensation and work-scheduling practices that will benefit frontline employees. Describing how the change would affect Maria, a 40-year-old mother and sales clerk in a retail store, will energize colleagues more quickly than talking about compensation for employees in general—at least when you are getting that conversation started. You can move into levels of abstraction later. The same thing goes for focusing on the well-being of Mike, a single parent, and his three school-aged children when arguing for programs that enhance broadband access—rather than talking about the amorphous community that needs internet access.

This is the approach that Kate Judson has taken at Adobe, where she is director of global onboarding, as she has worked to institutionalize hybrid work arrangements to enable employees to work from home, in the office, or in some combination. Remote work became accepted during the pandemic, but now many companies are mandating that employees return to the office. Kate does not want to see a return to the past. She believes that flexibility about where employees work not only leads to a more diverse and equitable workforce but is simply good business. As she sees it, allowing remote work for all, including working mothers, is good for employees *and* the bottom line. It allows companies to benefit from a much broader talent pool.

To make the case to executives, she tells stories about individual contributors who are working remotely and making a big impact. Kate uses her storytelling skills, along with her design expertise, to present case studies. I recently saw a short PowerPoint she had prepared for an internal presentation. Each slide featured a photo of an employee and a headline that summarized an accomplishment that the person had achieved, such as securing a big client. She also noted the employee's remote work location. She didn't make an abstract argument for hybrid work. With stories of real people and real accomplishments, she guided her audience to focus on impacts, not on whether this contributor was in the office or working from home.

▶ TELL YOUR OWN STORY

When you are thinking about stories that help make the case for change, don't forget your own.

Carmine Gallo, author of *The Storyteller's Secret*, believes your personal passion is the starting point for your story. It's not surprising, then, that the first secret in his book is this: "Inspiring storytellers are inspired themselves. They are very clear on their motivation, on the passion that drives them, and they enthusiastically share that passion with their audiences."[2]

If you don't care about the story you are telling, your audience won't care either.

Neil Giacobbi is a communications expert who understands the power of stories. After working in the world of public advocacy and political campaigns, he was recruited to join AT&T's public affairs department to represent the company to political, business, and civic leaders and to run public engagement campaigns.

He led the development of a national campaign, supported by AT&T, to combat cyberbullying. Stories were at the heart of the initiative. Working with teen filmmakers across the U.S., the team created a documentary about the pernicious abuse that some teens experience online. Based on stories from teens about how online bullying affected their lives, the documentary was designed to educate parents, teachers, and students about how to address this crisis.

In addition to being a communications specialist, Neil is a parent of three, and he knew that bullying was not the only hazard that young people face online. Too much time on laptops and smartphones saps the creative energy of kids and ruins their sleep, since some children even wake in the night to check their phones. Social media taunts them with unrealistic views of other people's lives, and children suffer by comparison. For some, exposure to social media leads to depression and suicidal thoughts.

Neil figured out how to deploy parental controls on his children's phones to limit their access to social media and online gaming. But he wanted to go beyond helping his own family. Neil believed that AT&T could play a role in addressing the problem on a much larger scale.

As he thought about this possibility, he found himself telling company executives how he had used controls on his children's phones.

"It was kind of an aha moment for me," Neil said. "As I shared my story, people repeatedly asked for my help in setting these controls on their children's phones. They were amazed that I could open my phone right then and turn off my son's access to his camera. Or I could give him access to a social media or gaming platform and limit the amount of time he spent there. These conversations confirmed for me that the need for this education was great."

He began to wonder, if people who worked in the telecommunications business were not aware of tools within their reach, how could others be expected to figure out these controls on their own? "I asked myself, what if we could get the salespeople in our retail stores to extend the support they provide to customers, to go beyond the initialization of the phone and offer parents training on the parental controls that are already built into the phone's operating system?"

As more and more of his colleagues recognized the need for this advice, they became increasingly interested in having AT&T play a key role in educating parents and caregivers on how to use these techniques effectively.

"The stories and the help I provided were like a foot in the door," Neil said. "They were essential for helping me get buy-in to run a pilot in select stores. We would train sales reps to provide guidance to parents, grandparents, or other caregivers who were purchasing a first phone for a child on how to activate parental controls."

Getting approval for the pilot was helped by the possible long-term benefit of the program to AT&T. It turned out that about one-third of the customers coming into the retail stores (pre-pandemic) were either buying the first phone for a child or buying a new phone for themselves and passing their older phone along to a child. Valuing the service they received while they were in the stores could turn them—and their children—into loyal customers for AT&T.

▶ **GIVE DATA A SUPPORTING, NOT STARRING, ROLE**
Stories helped Neil get the go-ahead for the pilot, but then he needed to convince the sales reps who resisted taking on this added responsibility. "They were reluctant because providing this additional training

to customers would take time away from selling phones or accessories or upscaling a customer's data plan, the activities that determined their compensation," Neil recalled. "I realized that I would have to change my pitch. A story just about the impact of the change wasn't going to do it."

So he studied the in-store experience and learned more about how the reps did their jobs. He learned that there was another critical factor in determining what sales reps were paid: customer satisfaction (CSAT) scores. These are calculated from those brief surveys that we as customers are asked to complete after receiving service from a rep.

So Neil and his team built a study of CSAT scores into the pilot and showed that the scores increased when sales reps offered this specific guidance to customers. Bingo.

Now Neil could bolster his story about the need for the service with data that made a compelling case for the sales teams.

▶ AIM FOR SIMPLICITY

When you craft a story, leave everything out but the essentials.

Be ruthless. We fall in love with our words (don't I know it!), but much of what you think has to be included in your story must fall onto the cutting-room floor.

Lin-Manuel Miranda, who created *Hamilton*, a Broadway sensation, is as good a storyteller as you can get. In his funny and riveting 2016 commencement address to University of Pennsylvania graduates, he told the audience, "The simple truth is that every story you choose to tell by necessity omits others from the larger narrative."[3] To tell a coherent and compelling story, you have to be selective.

It is hard to go for brevity when we try to communicate complicated ideas, especially when we have deep expertise in the subject. We want to explain the context, tell the history, explore the nuances. Taking time to get very clear about what you need the audience to know—and, importantly, what you want them to remember—will help you do the necessary editing. Nobody wants to hear, and nobody will remember, a story that doesn't deliver a succinct, powerful message.

I still remember a video used by a Fellow working in the area of human rights. The video uses animated characters and no words at all.[4]

It tells the story of a laborer who signs a contract for work and leaves his pregnant wife and child for a job that he thinks promises a better life. But the reality is quite different. He crosses a border, surrenders his passport, and finds that his wages must be used to pay for tools and transportation, housing and food. There is no way home. In less than a minute and a half, the video powerfully communicates what it means to be lured into a job and trapped into forced labor.

With just a few images, the video conveys the essence of forced labor, raises multiple questions, and can open the door to conversations about possible solutions.

That is the power of a simple, carefully crafted story.

▶ FACE UP TO YOUR OWN VERBOSITY

Most of us are willfully unaware that we talk much longer than we realize. That is true in meetings, on phone calls, and on the stage. Before the days of Zoom calls, Microsoft Teams, and Google Hangouts, in my office we used a conference call service that gave us a recap after each call on how much time each person spoke during the meeting. It was eye-opening, but certainly not surprising for the introverts on the call.

Over the years, I have participated in countless panel discussions and have listened to many more. Almost without exception, I have observed that people run over their allotted time slots. Most people think they will speak for, say, five minutes, but they go on for much longer—oblivious to the clock. So much for the interactive session that we were promised at the opening of the discussion.

Therefore, one way we help Fellows learn how to tell effective stories is by imposing strict time limits. We let them know how much time they have; and then when they start to speak, we set a timer and interrupt when the buzzer rings.

I am completely comfortable with those seemingly rude interventions now, but when I first joined the Aspen Business & Society Program, I struggled.

Early on, I was asked to serve as rapporteur for a dialogue we were hosting for C-suite executives. To set the stage for the discussions, each executive was invited to respond to this prompt: *Tell a story about a difficult challenge you are currently wrestling with that relates to business and trust.* They had a five-minute limit.

I was supposed to ring a chime and tell these senior executives that their time was up. My stress level rose. My shyness and sense of rank got in my way. I managed to ring the chime (very quietly!) but not to intervene. Several participants droned on. Audience attention drifted. The point of stories got lost.

Since then, I have facilitated dozens of dialogues and grown much more assertive. Brevity is good not only for the group, but also for the storyteller. When participants know they won't be subjected to stories without end or a clear point, they listen. And when storytellers know they have only a limited time to communicate their message, they tend to be much better prepared to deliver it.

▶ STUDY GREAT STORYTELLING—AND PRACTICE

As my interest in storytelling for business leaders has increased, I have found it fascinating to watch the TED phenomenon emerge. TED Talks are typically 20 minutes or less, and few presenters would dare walk onto the TED stage without rigorous preparation—often with the guidance of a highly paid consultant. Presenters need to learn how to make every word count in the time available.

Watching the TED Talks that have proven to be the most popular with audiences and thinking about why they work is like taking a master's-level course in storytelling. Listen to some of those talks and note the structure of each. What is the first sentence? The last sentence? What is the primary story that each TED presenter is telling? How many key points are they making? Ask yourself what message you remembered when the speaker was finished. Deconstruct these talks to see what techniques they use—humor, suspense, thoughtful repetition? Then think about how you deploy these techniques in your own presentations.

And for more in-depth insights on storytelling, I recommend *Made to Stick: Why Some Ideas Survive and Others Die.* Chip Heath and Dan Heath, masterful storytellers themselves, provide actionable advice for those who want to tell stories that are understood, are remembered, and have a lasting impact.[5] (Their first principle for storytelling, by the way, is simplicity—a point I emphasized earlier in this chapter.)

Use these tools to craft your own story, and then practice it (and time yourself!) until it flows.

Mario Juarez, a master storyteller who was communications director for Microsoft for many years, underscores how essential practice is for speakers. "Athletes and musicians who look like they're performing spontaneously have in fact dedicated thousands of hours to perfecting their crafts. Storytelling is no different. I tell clients that if they've got 10 minutes to deliver a critical presentation for an executive or big customer, they must practice it—completely—at least a dozen times before the event."[6]

▶ INVITE OTHERS TO TELL THEIR STORIES
In 2012, Nicola Acutt, then director of VMware's foundation, wanted to test a new idea for a service-learning experience that would enhance employees' leadership skills and deepen their appreciation for the role that business plays in achieving positive change in society. It was an ambitious goal for a five-day immersive program, but she pulled it off in part by making storytelling a central part in that effort.

Nicola had already converted the company's fairly typical corporate volunteering program into a service-learning experience: employees were assigned to small teams to work on projects in different parts of the world where they could use their business skills. Stories played a part in this early program. In exchange for being allowed to take five days off from work to participate, each employee was required to write a summary of what the experience had been like for them and what they learned.

"These stories were incredibly moving," Nicola told me. "Gratitude for the opportunity to participate was the number one theme we saw in the stories. Humility was another. They had a different view of the world. It was not the kind of learning you typically get in work assignments."

Being in the First Movers Fellowship provided an impetus for Nicola to ramp up these experiences further. "I wanted to be more intentional about using these short-term assignments to build greater leadership capacity. VMware already offered excellent classroom-based leadership training courses that taught you how to build a team, for example. But I thought these service-learning assignments could create opportunities for people to develop other critical leadership skills, like a global mindset, how to build trust on a diverse team, and to recognize and appreciate the strengths of others. Requiring them to tell their stories helped them synthesize and understand the power of reflection as a leadership tool."

Nicola got the go-ahead to test a pilot program. She accompanied five employees to work on a project in an orphanage in Kenya. They were to build a small computer lab and create a curriculum for teaching basic computer skills to local teachers.

From the start, Nicola wanted to be sure that participants had a chance to capture and tell the story of their experience. "I created a journal," she said. "I remember that I went to Kinko's the night before I was flying out to print copies for the group. It was a little bound book, and I had put a bunch of quotes throughout to prompt their thinking."

And she created space for participants to use the journal. "Each evening I asked them a different question to think about during the day, and then we would discuss it the next evening after dinner as we sat around the table in the orphanage where we were staying." She would ask, for example: What stood out for you today? What did you observe? They kept a record of their responses in the journals.

The storytelling continued on the trip back to Palo Alto. "I asked them to write the headline of the story they would tell when they returned to the office. I wanted them to be prepared to respond thoughtfully when their boss asked, 'How was your trip to Kenya?' and not to default to saying, for example, that the experience was awesome but they felt so sorry for the orphans and the poverty they observed."

Back home, there was an additional storytelling assignment. "Every participant had to prepare a presentation about their experience," Nicola explained. "Working with a designer, we offered a workshop to strengthen their storytelling skills."

It is perhaps easy to see reasons for the importance of building skills as a storyteller. But what does storytelling have to do with corporate social intrapreneurship?

Nicola believes there is a direct connection. "I'm confident that every one of the participants came out of the program with a very different perspective on the role of business in society and the potential that business has to be a partner in solving complex social problems," she said. "Storytelling helped them reflect on and define that possibility."

You may not have thought storytelling was a skill you needed to achieve change in your organization. In fact, it can be one of your most powerful levers. In *The Storyteller's Secret*, Carmine Gallo makes a bold claim: "Learn to tell a story, and your life and the lives of those you touch will be radically transformed."[7]

By preparing a story and telling it, we process and articulate what we have learned. And you can invite others to do the same.

Stories help people see both the need for change and the impact of change more quickly and more compellingly than facts and figures. As Margaret Renkl, an American essayist who writes regularly about nature, politics, and culture, observed, "We are convinced when we are moved much more often than we are convinced when we are informed."[8]

Impactful Collaborating

No one can whistle a symphony.
It takes an orchestra to play it.

—H. E. LUCCOCK

CHAPTER 7

Engage to Spark Collaboration

I frequently hear corporate social intrapreneurs say their work can feel like a lonely endeavor. In fact, a narrative has emerged that they are lone wolves. It is certainly true that when you see a new opportunity to create value for your company by addressing a thorny social or environmental problem, not many others are likely to share your vision, at least initially.

So in the early stages, when you have no idea whether there are others within your company ready to help you drive change, you can feel very much alone. However, many intrapreneurs have found, to their relief, that if you reach out to others, ask for their insights, and ignite their willingness to solve big challenges, many colleagues want to get involved. Intrapreneurs also discover that these allies bring valuable expertise and fresh perspectives that lead to better outcomes.

We can learn more about how this kind of collaboration works from Amy Edmonson, a Harvard Business School professor who studies a phenomenon she calls "teaming on the fly." By that she means "coordinating and collaborating with people across boundaries of all kinds, expertise, distance, time zones . . . to get work done."[1] In a popular TED Salon, she cited examples, such as the teams that come together in emergency rooms to save people's lives, the hundreds of diverse specialists who team up to produce animated films, and the cross-industry experts who work on huge initiatives, like figuring out how to build smart cities.

In these circumstances, she said, you "have to get different expertise at different times. You don't have fixed roles. You don't have fixed deliverables." She contrasted this kind of teaming with sports teams, where the same individuals practice the same strategies together over and over.

When you team on the fly, she explained, "you are going to be doing a lot of things that you haven't done before, and you can't do it in a stable team." This kind of ad hoc teaming, she continued, is "especially needed for work that is complex and unpredictable and for solving complex problems."

That sounds just like the situations faced by many corporate social intrapreneurs. There is no team already in place to tackle the wicked problem they want to solve. They must work across departments and functional capabilities, identify the expertise they need, and offer their own.

First Mover Fellows have taken various approaches to engaging others, as the examples below illustrate.

Meeting a Market Need

Feeding the world's growing population will require a significant increase in crop production, but challenges faced by small farmers around the world inhibit their ability to increase their crop yields and improve their livelihoods. Several years ago, Josh Henretig, then working in sustainability at Microsoft, and another colleague who worked in research were wondering how they could apply Microsoft's expertise in artificial intelligence (AI) and cloud computing to address these challenges.

In the face of severe water shortages, pollution, and unpredictable weather conditions, these farmers needed data to manage their land more effectively. Although drone imaging and sensor technologies existed to collect useful data that would help farmers use their land more productively and profitably, the cost of this technology was beyond their reach. Moreover, in many places, farmers didn't have access to the internet or weren't sufficiently savvy about technology to take advantage of these tools.

Neither Josh nor his colleague had all the expertise needed to overcome these challenges. However, they learned that a talented Microsoft engineer, Ranveer Chandra, was already investigating the use of digital technologies in agriculture. They saw a perfect opportunity for teaming up.

Although Josh didn't bring engineering expertise to the challenge, he knew he could play a critical collaborative role. Working across multiple teams, including Sustainability, Research, Engineering, and Corporate Affairs, he developed a shared project plan to present to management and secured a small seed investment to run an early-stage pilot. With that support, Ranveer Chandra and colleagues were able to deploy cost-effective technologies that helped farmers make better decisions to increase their crop yields and reduce natural resource consumption.

In one solution, for example, the team figured out how to take advantage of the unused spectrum between TV stations known as white space, abundantly available in rural areas, to transfer data collected from in-ground sensors to the cloud. With these data, combined with powerful algorithms, they created heat maps that farmers could use to help predict weather patterns and soil conditions. This information allowed farmers to make more informed decisions, like knowing when to apply fertilizer that works best on moist soil.

What started as a conversation between colleagues and outreach to an in-house expert grew into a pilot that has become an established program at Microsoft called FarmBeats, part of the company's effort to enable data-driven farming. It is now part of AI for Earth, a program Josh helped establish at Microsoft in 2017, which offers grants and technical support to individuals and organizations that use Microsoft cloud and AI tools to solve environmental problems. There is much more work to do, including making these applications even more affordable for the poorest farmers around the world, but the potential is huge. As Bill Gates wrote, "When most people think of groundbreaking digital technology, they don't picture soil sensors. But a farmer who knows the temperature, pH, and moisture level of his soil can make all sorts of informed decisions that save money and boost yield."[2]

Reconciling Competing Priorities

For JoAnn Stonier, teaming up meant ensuring that the legal team at Mastercard collaborated effectively with the business units.

Trained as a lawyer with expertise in data protection and privacy, JoAnn was hired by Mastercard in 2008 to update and oversee the credit card company's global privacy and protection program. Her task was not a small one, considering the billions of electronic payment transactions that Mastercard processes every day in more than 200 countries. Anybody who has been the victim of a data breach or had their credit card information stolen understands the critical importance of her role within the company.

To succeed, JoAnn had to champion both business growth and consumer protection. Finding the right balance required intrapreneurial vision and determination—and deft engagement with colleagues.

To make matters more challenging, she and her team worked in a domain that was evolving with breakneck speed. Credit card companies contended with changing, complex privacy laws and regulations, which differed country by country. Meanwhile, consumers were demanding that businesses effectively manage data and protect personal privacy. The consequences of getting it wrong were huge: loss of trust, revenues, and profits; fines; and a sustained hit to share price.

At the same time, the ability to collect and mine massive amounts of data gave credit card companies unprecedented, lucrative business development opportunities.

JoAnn knew that she and her team had to walk a fine line. They had to protect the data entrusted to the company while being responsive to their colleagues' desire to take advantage of the wealth of information available and stay competitive in the marketplace. "In effect," she said, "my team was basically injecting a new risk management system, but we couldn't be effective if we simply said no to opportunities." Her success depended on her ability to work collaboratively with her colleagues to be adaptive to the distinct needs of each of the teams they worked with.

To inform colleagues of what was possible in a new era of data regulations, and to learn what opportunities existed throughout the company, JoAnn and her team held "pizza and privacy" gatherings—with food as a lure. They also hosted events with cocktails and conversation, which they cheekily labeled "private affairs." In the arcane world of data and privacy,

JoAnn and her team showed that they had a sense of humor.

Rather than opening these affairs with a presentation telling business colleagues what they couldn't do in the current regulatory environment, JoAnn started with a focus on their needs. "Here is what I understand you are trying to do," she began. Only after acknowledging colleagues' needs did she talk about what the law allowed and how they might adapt their offerings to accommodate the privacy issues. As JoAnn explained, "We sought to come up with a new way together." These meetings, she said, became "privacy by design sessions."

This approach has gained real traction within the company. "A hall-mark of my success," JoAnn reflected, "is that my team is now invited in as new products and services are being envisioned at the company. We have a seat at the table from the beginning, so we are able to help create opportunities that balance the needs of business and society." In an area as complex as data privacy and, more broadly, data governance, being in these conversations is critical. In 2018, JoAnn became chief data officer at Mastercard. Still in culinary engagement mode, she began hosting "data and doughnuts" sessions to continue her work to achieve a great result for the business and protect consumer interests.

Tapping into the Lived Experience of Employees

When Zack Langway led the communications for the Office of the Chief Medical Officer at Johnson & Johnson, he was also a member of the company's Open & Out Employee Resource Group (ERG), an active network of nearly 5,000 employees in chapters around the globe who identify as LGBTQIA or who are allies of that community.

ERGs, now common, enable employees who share a particular identity (gender, ethnicity, religious affiliation, lifestyle, etc.) to connect. Although many ERGs serve as meaningful networking opportunities, they often have no direct impact on the operations of the company. Zack saw an opportunity for the Open & Out ERG to do more.

He wanted to tap into the group's expertise to help Johnson & Johnson better address health inequities and the underserved health needs of the LGBTQIA community.

These needs are many. Smoking rates among LGBTQIA people, for example, are higher than in the general population. As a result, they experience higher rates of smoking-related illnesses and deaths. The prevalence of depression, suicidal thoughts, and feelings of isolation is also disproportionately high, yet LGBTQIA-affirming mental health services are often inadequate.

For transgender individuals, the inequities are particularly significant. As Zack noted, "50 to 70 percent of trans folks report having to teach their own providers about how to care for them, and two-thirds of medical and surgical residents say that they don't know anything about gender confirmation surgery. They couldn't even describe it to you."

In the consumer products domain as well, the LGBTQIA community is not well served. Most childcare products, for example, are still marketed with a "traditional" family structure in mind, even though family structures have become much more diverse.

What do these disparities have to do with Johnson & Johnson? Plenty, as it turns out, given the company's product mix. For starters, the company sells Nicorette, a leading product to help people beat cravings and stop smoking. Johnson & Johnson also sells the Aveeno line of baby products. And Johnson & Johnson manufactures medical devices and surgical materials used for gender confirmation surgery.

Zack saw an opportunity to bring together people within the Open & Out ERG and form an internal think tank to consider ways that Johnson & Johnson could better serve the needs of this community. He tested his idea with leaders of two businesses where he thought he could make early progress: Nicorette and Aveeno. Both leaders agreed to try this new approach, which gave Zack confidence that he could productively engage Open & Out members.

Many members enthusiastically attended preliminary discovery sessions, where they were asked to reflect on the concept of sharing with the business insights on health inequities in the LGBTQIA community and their own experiences in the health care system.

Then, Zack recalled, "they looked at the ideas from the perspective of the business leads and asked themselves: What about these ideas will excite or motivate or inspire our business leaders the most? What questions will leaders have that we need to be prepared to answer? What will the business leads need in order to partner on this kind of a project?"

Zack went on to host additional sessions to reflect on more systemic topics, such as root causes of inequities in health. "We challenged ourselves to consider what is Johnson & Johnson's right to play in this space," Zack explained, "and considered what makes us a credible actor. We thought about how our unique positioning, combined with LGBTQIA employees' lived insights, could make 'pie in the sky' ideas actionable—and how different resources at the company could be combined to bring some of these ideas to life."

These early conversations led to the development of Open & Out LABS.

LABS is in its early stage, but it has already shown that engaging people to share their lived experiences and putting colleagues' personal passions toward what might be possible for their own communities' health is energizing for all. If LABS delivers on its promise, it could help the company develop new products that would do well in the market *and* lead to better health outcomes for the LGBTQIA population. "Beyond that," Zack said, "I believe that if the Open & Out LABS is successful, it could serve as a model for engaging with other ERGs, at this company and well beyond."

Good for the business. Good for society. And achieving change at the level of the system. That is an intrapreneur's dream.

Creating a Shared Narrative

When you are trained in sustainability and hired to be the sustainability professional in a company with a purpose rooted in sustainable principles, you may think it will be smooth sailing. No intrapreneurial skills required. You just do what you have been mandated to do.

As we have seen in many other stories throughout this book, that is rarely the case. Achieving change in companies of all kinds is complicated work, as Drummond Lawson realized when he was hired as greenskeeping manager at Method Products Inc. after completing his degree in chemistry and environmental science.

Method seemed like the perfect place to work for someone with his expertise. Founded in 2000 by two childhood friends, the company challenged the way cleaning products were typically made: with hazardous chemicals, offensive odors, and wasteful, ugly packaging primarily designed to dominate the shelves of supermarkets. Method went up against the big guys, like Procter & Gamble, Clorox, and Dial, and managed to carve out an important market niche. (Method was acquired by S. C. Johnson in 2017 and retains its commitment to sustainability.)

Ironically, Drummond realized, the company's strong environmental orientation seemed to stifle further investment in sustainability. As he told me, people were inclined to believe, "We're already doing our part."

Despite advances in green chemistry that offered new safe and effective ingredients, brand managers hesitated to approve changes to formulations or packaging that might threaten their commercial success. And when new formulations were used, the sales team was often intimidated by the complexity of the environmental claims and relied on generic messaging such as "eco-friendly." This lack of boldness contributed to a drop in revenues—the first the brand had ever experienced—as the dominant cleaning brands launched their own greener product lines.

Drummond wondered if he could design a collaborative learning journey with colleagues to uncover what he called "the logic of what we were trying to do in our products and throughout the supply chain." Articulating this logic, he thought, could help colleagues better understand the company's sustainability stories and the opportunities in this space that still lay ahead. If competitors were copying elements of their greener formulations, they would have a much harder time copying the depth of the practices in Method's operations.

Working with Method's design team, he settled on three core questions: What do we make? How do we make it? And why do we believe that's important? Colleagues interested in these questions gathered in design sessions over several months to find answers.

The discovery process gave employees a clearer, more holistic view of what differentiated Method from the competition. They became better equipped to tell a more compelling story about the company. "Not only could we claim that we made our products with lower-impact ingredients and made our bottles out of completely recycled plastic," Drummond explained. "We shifted the conversation from simplistic product attributes to the values and beliefs that underlay the design process and ultimately the company."

When I visited Method's headquarters in San Francisco some years ago, Drummond showed me where this team met for discovery sessions. A graphic designer had created a map of all of the brand's sustainability efforts, reflected in stickies posted on the whiteboards and shaped into a visual communications architecture. This visualization of the Method story eventually became the "Greenskeeping Tool Kit" used by sales and marketing teams and won an award from AIGA, the professional association for design.

What did this work mean for the company? One clear result, Drummond said, was that it built confidence within the organization to explain the brand value more effectively to retailers (who had the power to position the products on their shelves) and to the public. Method's approach to sustainability differed from others'. For example, Method eschewed bland packaging and colorless formulations that retailers and consumers had come to associate with environmentally friendly products. Instead, Method's products and packaging were distinctive in their bold colors, designs, and fragrances. These aspects were designed for mass appeal—the Trojan horse to bring category-leading environmental innovation into the aisles of mass retailers.

Once Method's sales team and others understood the research behind the design process, they were ready to convince a skeptical market that they could have effective, clean products—and cool designs too. It was a win-win for consumers and the planet.

Pointers for Engaging Effectively

As the stories from Josh, JoAnn, Zack, and Drummond show, there are many kinds of challenges that are best tackled by working collaboratively with colleagues. If you seek to engage, here are some pointers for achieving success.

▶ EMBRACE CURIOSITY TO LEARN FROM OTHERS

Successful collaborations depend on curiosity. According to Amy Edmondson, it is a key variable that differentiates successful teams from others. The participants in successful teams demonstrate humility in the face of challenges and are genuinely curious about the expertise that others bring to problem-solving.

Passion and empathy are also critical. "Curiosity drives people to find out what others know, what they bring to the table, what they can add," Edmondson writes. "Passion fuels enthusiasm and effort. It makes people care enough to stretch, to go all out. Empathy is the ability to see another's perspective, which is absolutely critical to effective collaboration under pressure."[3]

Fellows have learned that no matter how enthusiastic you are about your idea for a product, service, business model, or business practice that you want your company to embrace, the probability of your idea alone being the best one is virtually zero. You need to bring others in and be prepared to learn from them.

Rejecting the accepted norms and practices, as intrapreneurs do, is not the end of the story. The most successful of them don't lock into a fixed notion about how to move forward. They realize that seeking input from others doesn't slow you down. It makes your idea better.

Zack Langway, for example, reached out to employees and business leaders as he formulated an approach for moving forward. With each conversation, the concept of tapping into the expertise of employees to develop better products and enhance health outcomes became more layered and actionable. In all cases, Zack intentionally invited people in to cocreate, not to validate. When he was ready to launch the Open & Out LABS, he already had buy-in and engagement from many key players.

▶ SEE YOURSELF AS A CATALYST

Corporate change agents often function as sparks that trigger an organizational reaction.

In reflecting on his experience at Method, Drummond Lawson said that the role of the corporate social intrapreneur is "to set the stage and help others create the arguments to overcome barriers and help with technical issues when needed. The role is less about ownership and more about influencing and coordinating." He quipped, "In fact, once you do a very good job as an intrapreneur in setting the stage, you don't have to have any good ideas!"

I think it's unlikely that Drummond Lawson, an environmental chemist who is fluent in three languages and proficient in two others, and who, by his own description, is an overly competitive downhill skier and long-distance biker, will ever stop generating innovative ideas once he gets others engaged. However, I am confident that the quantity and quality of ideas increased at Method when Drummond initiated the discovery journey with his colleagues.

▶ SHARE THE JOY OF PROBLEM-SOLVING

Working as a catalyst, you have the opportunity to bring others into the "problem-solving tent." That's exactly what Josh Henretig did at Microsoft.

He was not an engineer, and he knew engineers were in very high demand at his company, and very busy. However, by offering an opportunity to work on a problem that really mattered in the world, Josh got the attention of highly skilled and sought-after talent. "Engineers love to solve problems," he explained. "It turns out that many love to solve problems so much that when they aren't on a specific work assignment, they are willing to use some of their time to tackle other big ones. There is a higher calling for engineers who want to be connected to some part of positive change."

In assembling a problem-solving team, Josh demonstrated what Deborah Ancona and Hal Gregersen, leadership experts at the Massachusetts Institute of Technology (MIT), call "challenge-driven leadership." Unlike more traditional models of leadership, in which leaders are motivated by authority or status, challenge-driven leadership attracts people who want to solve problems and have expertise and creativity to offer. Such leaders "excel at choreographing and directing the work of others, because their expert knowledge enables them to spot opportunities to innovate in a way that cannot be done by working alone," write Ancona and Gregersen.[4]

These professors uncovered this leadership approach as they sought to explain how MIT students and alumni have achieved such a stunning amount of innovation. According to a study by the Kauffman Foundation, "MIT alumni have launched more than 30,200 active companies that collectively employ roughly 4.6 million people and generate roughly $1.9 trillion in annual revenues."[5]

This kind of leadership, Ancona and Gregersen assert, is needed "where innovation and entrepreneurship are required—and in particular, where developing a solution requires drawing together diverse talents and perspectives to discover novel approaches."[6]

The challenge-driven leadership that Ancona and Gregersen describe is exactly what I have seen intrapreneurs do over and over. They bring the challenge to the right people and marshal their expertise and passions. They build a team that can solve tough problems and deliver business value.

A key lesson for all corporate social intrapreneurs is that there is likely to be far more capacity and interest within your company to work on the problem that matters to you than you initially realize. When you use your institutional knowledge to find people with special expertise and invite them to help solve a problem, you stand a much better chance of influencing change in your company.

▶ BE WILLING TO LET GO AND GIVE OTHERS THE CREDIT

When you have worked—sometimes for years—to build engagement around an idea for change and the idea takes off, it can be very difficult to hand over control to others. One Fellow remarked that for a long time he had advised making changes to the company's fleet of vehicles to achieve both environmental and business benefits. But people clung to the old way—until the benefits became evident to them. "Now," this Fellow said, "everybody wants to play in my sandbox."

You could be forgiven for wanting to shout, "I told you so!" or "Remember, this was my idea!" But you have to keep the longer-term picture in mind and realize that without widespread engagement, the idea would probably not have come to fruition. Or it would have been a flash in the pan.

The real victory for corporate social intrapreneurs is when the product, service, business model, or practice is fully integrated into the way the company operates. Then it becomes everybody's success story. That's the kind of enduring change you want.

The mind works best
in the presence of a question.

—NANCY KLINE, *MORE TIME TO THINK*

CHAPTER 8

Inquire with Questions
That Ignite Imaginations

Felipe Botero, a self-described technologist, worked in insurance for over three decades, much of that time at MetLife. While there, he was the professional who knew how to keep the systems running so that policyholders' data were stored and protected, premiums were collected, and policy redemptions were made promptly and accurately.

Felipe loved the insurance business and the IT infrastructures that allow it to thrive. But throughout his years in the business, he was driven by another professional passion as well: microinsurance.

As he gained expertise in the industry, he realized the potential for MetLife to move into this new market segment—to provide responsible and affordable insurance products to low-income people around the globe. Typically, insurance companies offer products that serve customers at the higher end of the income scale, but Felipe believed microinsurance would offer a path for profitable growth for MetLife and help raise the standard of living for many people whose livelihoods are constantly threatened by the consequences of a catastrophic event.

That passion came from his own life experience. Felipe was born in Colombia. When he was eight years old, his father died. As he recalled, "That was a defining moment for me. Thankfully, my dad had a lot of foresight and had purchased a small insurance policy. With that money, my mother, now a widow who had never been employed and had five children under 10, was able to move us from Bogotá to New York City. She was able to make a down payment on a home in Queens—a very modest house, but that's the house we grew up in. And then she worked really hard as a customer service representative at an airport. She managed her finances to the penny, and she raised five kids—all of us now college graduates and working in executive positions at different companies.

"When I reflect on our success, I always go back to thinking about how critical it was for us to have that little bit of advantage—a small insurance policy—to rely on when my dad was unfortunately taken from us."

Persistently, over many months, Felipe raised the topic of this underserved market with his MetLife supervisors, his peers, and the corporate executives with whom he worked in his capacity as vice president of global technology and operations. They listened with detachment.

Then, Felipe said, "I had a big aha. I had been trying to move this innovation forward on my own, to have all the answers, to tell people about this great opportunity and this great emerging business opportunity with social impact. But then I realized that I didn't have to have all the answers, I just needed to have good questions. When people have answers to those questions, they become part of the solution. So I started to take a different approach."

From then on, when he met with colleagues, he no longer tried to sell the idea. Instead, he led with questions: What might an approach to this market look like? How is this market defined? What would have to happen for MetLife to move into this market?

"Over several years, we built a really good network of people who were also passionate about microinsurance," Felipe said. "They were very talented people who became engaged and looked forward to driving this idea forward." As a result, instead of a handful of people interested in these possibilities, dozens of people all over the world started imagining how to create new products that could provide life-changing resources to people everywhere.

Learning to Lead with Questions

Felipe's story could easily have been told in the previous chapter of this book as an example of cocreating and teaming. I have chosen to include it here because Felipe's aha moment rested on his realization of the central importance of questions in driving change.

Too often, questions get short shrift in stories of innovation. But in reality, they typically play a starring role. As Hal Gregersen, the longtime collaborator with Clayton Christensen and Jeff Dyer (a trio of innovation experts), asserts, if you "trace the origin story of any creative breakthrough, it is possible to find the point where someone changed the question."[1]

That is why in working with First Movers, we emphasize the transformative power of questions, and we help Fellows become better at crafting the kinds of questions that lead to breakthrough thinking.

In my own career, I wish I had learned this lesson earlier. I spent too much time trying to have the right answer.

As a banker, I needed answers—or so I thought—for my managers to know I was on top of the job content. I needed answers—or so I thought—for my clients to understand that I had a well-thought-out pitch to justify my sales call. I needed answers—or so I thought—for my colleagues to appreciate that I was a team player, more than able to hold up my end.

To a large extent, I was right. It's certainly important to build expertise, come prepared for meetings, and contribute to the team effort. But I didn't realize that having the right questions is also a way to demonstrate expertise, prepare, and contribute. My visits as a banker to corporate treasury offices would have been more productive if I had arrived with thoughtful questions that invited treasury staff to think more deeply about their needs and their goals. Rather, I came with a pitch and often with a product specialist poised to present an idea. That shifted the spotlight to us and away from discovering what the client really needed.

Especially since joining the Aspen Institute, I have come to have a much deeper understanding of the power of inquiry and the importance of inquiring with a deeply rooted intent to learn. I have also studied how to get better at crafting and asking questions that lead to breakthrough results—and I have seen Fellows make progress by deploying them. Below are some ideas for how to build that capacity.

▶ INQUIRE WITH HUMILITY

Edgar Schein, late professor emeritus at the MIT Sloan School of Management, communicated the importance of humility in his essential 110-page book, *Humble Inquiry: The Gentle Art of Asking Instead of Telling.*

Schein points out that in both our professional and personal lives, most of us default to asserting, advocating, and advising, instead of inquiring and inviting. He shows us the way to a different path, to embrace the practice of humble inquiry, "the fine art of drawing someone out, of asking questions to which you do not already know the answer, of building a relationship based on curiosity and interest in the other person."[2]

It takes a concerted effort to move off the default path of asserting, but the payoff is worth it. According to Schein, "What we choose to ask, when we ask, what our underlying attitude is as we ask—all are key to relationship building, to communication, and to task performance."[3]

Effective corporate social intrapreneurs have learned the art of balancing expertise and humble inquiry. But it can be a challenge. After all, intrapreneurs generally rely on their content and functional expertise to imagine approaches to solving social and environmental challenges. They are experts in their fields and want to communicate this expertise to others to help make their case.

Technology experts, for example, may already have an informed view of what needs to change to ensure that products and processes are more inclusively designed. Human rights specialists know what it takes to build a practice of ethical sourcing. Financial innovators know how to structure a social impact offering to go to market. In all of these cases, and many more, however, the prospects of achieving the change they seek will be enhanced by inviting the input of others, by inquiring with humility.

▶ RECOGNIZE THAT ALL QUESTIONS ARE NOT CREATED EQUAL

Few of us think about the need to build question-asking capability. After all, we ask questions all the time. Just think about how many questions you type into the Google search box every day. But the kinds of questions that ignite innovation and fresh thinking on tough challenges are not ones that can be answered by a Google search.

To take advantage of the transformative power of questions requires that we become students of questions and learn how to craft them.

My understanding of question crafting took a giant leap forward many years ago when I was introduced to the concept of Appreciative Inquiry by two leading scholars in the field, David Cooperrider and Ronald Fry from Case Western Reserve University.

Appreciative Inquiry, which I referenced in chapter 3, is about "the search for the best in people, their organizations, and the strengths-filled, opportunity-rich world around them."[4] It is an approach to personal, organizational, or systems change that rests on discovering strengths rather than deficits. This approach is rooted in what Appreciative Inquiry practitioners call "unequivocally positive" questions, ones designed to uncover strengths in the system on which to build future opportunities for growth and improvement.

As the authors of the *Encyclopedia of Positive Questions* explain, this kind of question "brings out the best in people and organizations while amplifying and magnifying the most positive life-giving possibilities for the future."[5]

The *Encyclopedia* offers many examples of these kinds of questions. In a section of the book titled, "No Limits to Cooperation," the authors propose asking, "When have you had a sense of wonder, surprise, or delight because cooperation in this organization went beyond anticipated limits? Tell a story about this time."[6] In a section on performance, they suggest asking, "Put yourself in our customers' shoes. What do you think they would say if we asked them what makes this organization best in class?"[7] To discover more about how to create cultures that give companies a strategic advantage, the authors propose asking, "When you think of organizations that you consider the best employers in your community or profession, what is it about their culture that makes them attractive to you? How might we create more of that quality within our own culture?"[8]

Studying Appreciative Inquiry opened my eyes to the value of thinking very carefully about the kinds of questions we ask, and I have been on the lookout for additional insights ever since.

On that search I was delighted to discover Warren Berger's book *A More Beautiful Question: The Power of Inquiry to Spark Breakthrough Ideas.*

The inspiration for the title was a journal entry by the poet E. E. Cummings: "Always the beautiful answer who asks a more beautiful question."

Berger, trained as a journalist and now a self-described "questionologist," has been on a long quest to find beautiful questions, which he defines as "ambitious yet actionable," ones that "can begin to shift the way we perceive or think about something—and that might serve as a catalyst to bring about change."[9]

His book is filled with stories of times when a thoughtful question led to breakthrough ideas. Because I relied on typewriters throughout college and in the early years of my career (and made a lot of typing errors), I particularly enjoyed his story of Bette Nesmith Graham.

Graham was a secretary back in the 1950s who used an electric typewriter. She also did work as a commercial artist. One night, she asked herself a fateful question: What if I could paint over my mistakes when typing, the way I do when painting? She created a solution of paint and water that she could swipe on text to cover the error. When it dried, she could type over her mistake. With this invention, she went on to start a company eventually called Liquid Paper. Nowadays, working on our computers, we simply delete and retype. But during my college years, a swipe of this white liquid allowed me to correct errors and salvage many term papers. And I wasn't the only one who saw its value. In 1979, she sold the company to Gillette for nearly $50 million.[10] It all began with a question.

For more stories about transformative questions, peruse Berger's index of questions at the end of the book. It's a treasure trove.

Hal Gregersen's book *Questions Are the Answer* is another valuable source for understanding what he calls "catalytic" questions, ones that "dissolve barriers to thinking, like limiting prior assumptions, and they channel energy down new, more productive pathways."[11]

The chapters in Gregersen's book, appropriately titled as questions, take readers on a memorable journey to discover how questions can lead to breakthroughs not only in business but also in your personal life.

Positive, beautiful, and catalytic questions are a far cry from the gotcha questions that we often face—and sometimes direct at others: "Why can't you see the possibilities in this suggestion?" "How come you couldn't finish this assignment on time?" "Don't you think this plan is superior to what someone else proposed?" Learning the difference and making a conscious choice to avoid "questioning" someone can lead to much more productive conversations.

▶ FIND A GO-TO QUESTION

Years ago, long before the current explosion of interest in impact investing, Chris McKnett discovered his own positive, beautiful, catalytic question. At the time, Chris was working at State Street Global Advisors (SSGA), where he was attempting to develop a new product offering that would meet two market needs: low-income consumers needing credit and social impact investors seeking low-risk vehicles for investing in community development. Such products were difficult to structure and take to market, and he was running into dead ends with his colleagues. Everyone had thoughts about why such an investment vehicle wouldn't work. We have all heard these kinds of objections: The product was too complicated. The product was too niche. It was not the right time. The ideas had been tried in the past without success.

Finally, Chris (like Felipe in the story earlier in this chapter) decided to stop trying to persuade people to move forward. Instead, he turned to inquiry. In conversations with colleagues he asked, "What would have to be true for State Street to be able to structure and sell investment products that would meet these two market needs?"

Chris didn't immediately get answers that helped develop the product he sought. However, by asking what would have to be true, he learned a great deal about his institution's commitments to finding innovative solutions for investors and consumers and its capacities for creating these products. Also, he became better able to articulate these possibilities within the firm. Senior executives, including the CEO, sought insights from him, and he was asked to take on responsibility for designing and implementing a global sustainable and responsible investing policy that could serve as an overarching summary of SSGA's perspective and position. Several years later, he took on full responsibility for running the Environmental, Social, and Governance (ESG) group at SSGA. His efforts helped set it on the path for becoming a leader in ESG.

What was "right" about Chris's question—What would have to be true for us to be able to offer a product that would meet two specific market needs?—was that it ignited the imagination, a sense of possibilities, and aspirations among his colleagues. He used it repeatedly to see patterns and learn from others.

I have been intrigued by the go-to questions that I hear innovative leaders use. These questions, asked widely and repeatedly, can help you spot patterns and trends and allow you to build collective wisdom.

Amanda Billiot, a corporate social intrapreneur and vice president of human resources at Pratt & Whitney, consistently asks, "How can I help you?" Also, in the spirit of continuous improvement, she asks, "What should we stop doing, continue to do, or start doing?" She can't always act immediately on each recommendation, but by collecting insights from many employees, she is better able to set priorities and take action.

Matthew Breitfelder is head of human capital at Apollo Global Management, one of the largest private equity firms in the world. I have worked with him as a member of the First Movers Fellowship design team since the program was launched. I often recall a conversation we had years ago. He told me that he makes a habit of asking colleagues, "Why do you do the work that you do?" With this question, he invites people to talk about how they value their work and the purpose they see in it, in order to move away from a discussion about functional responsibilities, deadlines, and challenges.

Krista Tippett, host of the podcast *On Being* and recipient of the National Humanities Medal for "thoughtfully delving into the mysteries of human existence," notes that "What if . . ." was one of the questions repeatedly asked by people as diverse as Albert Einstein, who gave the world the theory of relativity, and John Lewis, a tireless advocate for civil rights.[12]

Corporate social innovators are also constantly asking this question—What if we were to expand our product offerings to include microinsurance products for a market that is currently underserved? What if we were able to design a financial product that delivers value for investors and creates social impact within the communities where the capital is invested? What if we wanted to ensure that principles of human rights are embedded at every stage of our supply chain?

126

And the what-if question is quickly followed by another powerful question: "How might we . . ."

These are essential inquiries for anyone trying to make deep change within complex systems.

▶ ASK FOLLOW-UP QUESTIONS

When you practice humble inquiry most effectively, you do not ask a question, hear the response, and then quickly take the opportunity to share your own thoughts. You ask follow-up questions that keep the space open for a real conversation to emerge. Harvard professors Alison Wood Brooks and Leslie John have found that "follow-up questions seem to have a special power. They signal to your conversation partner that you are listening, care, and want to know more."[13]

The good news for those learning how to craft better questions: follow-up questions are easy and short. For example, simply asking, "Can you tell me more?" prompts the speaker to continue to think and explain ideas more completely. Michael Bungay Stanier, a leadership coach, advocates for what he calls the AWE question: "And what else?"[14] He uses this question extensively with his coaching clients to good effect.

Build these questions into your inquiry lexicon, and you will be surprised by how they enrich your conversations at work—and at home.

▶ TRY A QUESTION BURST

To make progress in finding the right questions, Hal Gregersen teaches people how to do "question bursts." For this exercise, you begin by identifying a challenge that you are facing. You can do question bursts in pairs or gather a small group so that you can benefit from a variety of perspectives.

Here is how it works: You explain the challenge very briefly. Then, you launch a timed brainstorming session during which everyone generates as many questions as possible. As participants propose questions, you write them down. Gregersen recommends a four-minute session in which you aim to jot down 15 to 20 questions suggested by participants. (You are not allowed to answer any of these questions, nor is anyone allowed to provide context for their questions.) When the burst is finished, you can begin examining the questions and see if any of them help you see the challenge from another angle.[15]

This exercise is valuable for both you and the question generators. Everyone is energized by the collective question-crafting experience.

▶ BUILD A MEETING AGENDA BASED ON QUESTIONS

With Fellows we use a simple and effective exercise to help them learn how to craft questions: We ask them to think about a significant upcoming meeting with someone whose support they need to move their innovative ideas forward. Instead of preparing the meeting agenda based on bullet points and topics, the default approach for most of us, we ask them to build the agenda around questions.

We advise them to think of beautiful questions, to use Warren Berger's phrase, that will ignite the imagination and aspirations of the person they are meeting with. These questions should also be crafted to uncover possibilities and elicit information about strengths rather than weaknesses. Further advice about crafting these impactful questions comes from Jack Soos, another First Mover, who says, "I try to find the question that someone will remember when I leave the room." And we remind Fellows to build time into the agenda for follow-up questions.

When the Fellows have generated their questions, we have them pair up. They take turns briefly explaining whom they are going to meet with and why this meeting matters. Then they discuss the questions that each has drafted. These conversations are lively, and Fellows tell us that this exercise helps them take a fresh approach that leads to more productive meetings.

Nilofer Merchant, a noted innovator and influential management thinker, uses a similar approach when she prepares to run workshops on innovation and leadership. She takes a sheet of paper and writes down all of the ideas that would be useful for her to share in the meeting. On the other side of the paper, she writes questions she could pose that would help her learn more about others' motivations, emotions, and needs. Even if she doesn't use all the questions, preparing them ensures that she will be "primed to be curious."[16] And what she learns from inquiring helps her tailor her own inputs in the sessions.

Being "primed to be curious" in meetings and conversations of all kinds is an idea that can help you move your work forward. The next step is to learn to listen attentively to people's responses to your questions, as we'll discuss in the following chapter.

Wisdom is the reward you get
for a lifetime of listening
when you'd have preferred to talk.

—DOUG LARSON, COLUMNIST,
GREEN BAY PRESS-GAZETTE

CHAPTER 9

Listen to Learn

I f you were asked to identify synonyms for corporate social intrapreneurs, you would probably select action-oriented words: *Movers. Shakers. Change agents. Catalysts.* All are useful and accurate. However, a description that is apt but much less likely to come to mind is *expert listeners.*

When First Movers tell stories about how they drove change in their companies, we often hear the phrase, "The first thing I did was to listen."

Listening is foundational for achieving the change these intrapreneurs seek. It is essential for coalition building, cocreating, and collective problem-solving. As emphasized in chapter 8, such productive engagement is triggered by asking catalytic questions, the kind that ignite colleagues' imaginations and capabilities. However, committing to engage and learning to ask good questions is pointless if you aren't fully determined to listen to what others have to say and be changed by what you hear.

Most of us think we are pretty good listeners. Consequently, we don't dedicate time to learn how to get better. However, Nancy Kline, who studies listening, believes that most people have no idea how to give "attention of a generative quality," which she argues is essential for effective listening. Instead, she says, "most people think that listening is linear. They think listening is lined up waiting, waiting to speak."[1]

Mark Goulston, a psychiatrist and coach and the author of *Just Listen: Discover the Secret to Getting Through to Absolutely Anyone,* agrees. He says that to be a good listener, you have to let go of your desire to be interesting and start getting interested instead. "The first key," Goulston advises, "is to stop thinking of conversation as a tennis match. (He scored a point. Now I need to score a point.) Instead, think of it as a detective game, in which your goal is to learn as much about the other person as you can. Go into the conversation knowing that there is something very interesting about the other person, and be determined to discover it."[2]

When you are passionate about an idea, as corporate social intrapreneurs are, and you believe the need for change is urgent, as these intrapreneurs do, you may think the highest priority for moving your idea forward is to convince others of its validity and importance. As we saw in the previous two chapters, that approach rarely works. To be effective, changemakers must learn to balance their passion with a deep commitment to listen to and learn from others.

Nilofer Merchant puts it this way: When trying to persuade others to accept your idea, the approach of many is to "identify what key ideas could convince them. Find persuasive facts. Enthusiastically share. Beat their facts back with your facts." Instead, she asserts, "the best way is not to tell them *your* answer, but to arrive at *an* answer—together. Listening is the key pathway to go from *your* idea to *our* idea. To reshape the idea as needed, and to ultimately create the kind of shared ownership that is needed for any idea to become a new reality."[3]

Listening Is the First Step for Getting Buy-In

Dan Kim, with expertise in finance, strategy, and sustainable energy, has used a listen-first approach throughout his career.

Early on, as a young engineer, he had responsibility for managing a petrochemical business and employees who had more work experience than he did. Dan knew that his team had seen engineers like him come and go. The only way he was able to manage effectively and build trust was to listen and learn from this experienced group.

Later in his career, when Dan began to collaborate with companies focused on lowering the carbon footprint of the transportation sector, he called on his skill as a listener to learn and get the collective buy-in and ownership needed to drive change.

As chief financial officer at World Energy, a producer and distributor of biofuels, Dan was well served by the strategy of "listening first." World Energy used hydrogen to convert waste animal fat into renewable fuels for airplanes and trucks. The company was planning to increase its capacity fivefold and needed to work with diverse constituencies—suppliers, customers, investors, and policy makers—to get the plant built. "I knew I was far from the expert in these planning sessions," Dan explained. "Listening to people who had deeper expertise and experience and appreciating what others had to contribute is how I built consensus around the business model to advance the project." The plant is now being built to become one of the largest sustainable aviation fuel facilities in North America.

Then, at Pilot Company, one of the largest travel center networks in North America, Dan co-led the "disruptive fuels" team to drive development of sustainable alternative energy platforms. Again, by listening and learning from people who had operating expertise that he lacked, he was able to build credibility, drive change forward, and create innovative opportunities for his company. In partnership with the trucking team leadership, for example, Dan launched a hydrogen trucking business that will play a significant role in developing a hydrogen ecosystem in North America.

Now, as chief strategic officer at NEXT Renewable Fuels, Dan still places a premium on listening as he continues his work toward industry decarbonization. Dan believes you must consider every fuel option—including fossil fuels—to lower emissions substantially. There is no single silver bullet. "The full value chain is evolving," he said. "How do you effect that change? It's done by understanding the different views people bring to the market instead of dismissing or marginalizing people, especially from traditional oil, gas, or even coal."[4]

Listening can lead to all sorts of victories. One intrapreneur discovered he could defuse tensions on his team simply by taking time to hear people out rather than moving quickly into a how-do-we-fix-this-problem mindset. Another realized that her team was already brimming with energy to work for the change she hoped to achieve. She didn't need to inspire her direct reports; she just needed to give them a space to talk about what they wanted to accomplish, listen, and then give them leeway to act.

Similarly, years ago, when Jack Soos was given responsibility for running a business unit at Pratt & Whitney, he found that listening helped him overcome two major challenges. First, morale in the unit was low. Because of recent divestitures that affected the team, leadership had shifted its attention elsewhere. The unit wasn't getting adequate support from across the company or being recognized for their efforts. Second, his assignment required renegotiating Pratt & Whitney's contract with one remaining and significant customer. This customer relied on the company's jet engine technology to generate essential electric power, but it felt sidelined by the corporate reorganization. Conditions weren't ideal for contract renegotiations.

Jack understood that he couldn't begin to address either of these challenges without listening carefully to members of his team and to the customer. He sought first to learn from the employees—to understand how organizational changes were affecting the team and what they needed from management and from internal support groups to do their jobs well. By listening carefully, he also got an appreciation for their significant expertise and the pride these employees took in their work. Armed with these insights, he began advocating for this group within the company to get the services that the employees in this unit needed.

Then, to make sure that he thoroughly understood the customer's expectations, he set up office space at the customer's location and arranged with the leadership there to allow part of the Pratt & Whitney team to work alongside them a couple of days a week. There they could listen at close range.

The result of these efforts was good for the employees and good for business. Jack's willingness to listen to employees and advocate on their behalf changed the tone in the group. And the attention that he paid to rebuilding trust with the customer made it possible for him to renegotiate the contract so that they could more productively move forward together.

Mark Goulston's research supports the notion that listening leads to buy-in. As he writes, "Most people upshift when they want to get through to other people. They persuade. They encourage. They argue. They push. And in the process, they create resistance." Rather, Goulston suggests, you should "listen, ask, mirror, and reflect back to people what you've heard." When you do, "they will feel seen, understood, and felt—and that unexpected downshift will draw them to you."[5]

Listening Tours Generate Diverse Insights

Listening "tours" can be an excellent starting point for driving change. One of our Fellows used this approach to prompt more inclusive, gender-balanced decision-making at her company. The tour consisted of conversations with colleagues at all levels and in all departments to develop a vision for the company in 2030. The core question: What would have to be true for the company to be more inclusive of women's input?

These conversations produced more than 90 unique ideas for advancing inclusive decision-making.

In addition to generating ideas, the tour had a positive impact on participants. They said they felt honored to be included. Participants who came to these conversations out of a sense of duty were amazed at how engaged they felt—and how hopeful. "This is much more fun than my day job," said one. This kind of change comes more slowly than many of us hope, but the conversations created greater momentum for change and ignited latent energy within the company.

Listening tours can take you outside the company as well. When he was marketing director for renewables at General Electric, John Renehan faced the challenge of championing innovation for a nascent renewable energy business in a company with a 125-year history in energy, and not the renewable kind.

Practices and policies were firmly in place, and there was deep resistance to change. To gain a broader perspective on changing energy markets, John took his team outside of the company and around the world to seek input on a big question: What does the future of power look like? The team reached out to energy start-ups, employees, utility companies, venture capitalists—anyone who would have an informed perspective on what might lie ahead.

Their findings allowed them to open fresh conversations with colleagues, customers, and prospects that deepened their relationships. As a result of the insights gained, John's team was able to test various business models before recommending investment strategies to GE leadership. Moreover, the company gained a sales edge. Building on their findings, the team was emboldened to ask questions of their customers about trends that they would not have known to ask had they not gone on this listening tour.

Listening Removes Roadblocks

Sometimes listening simply makes it easier to find problems and solve them. Kaity Ruger was director of data at Aetna (now a CVS Health Care Company); she led a cross-functional team that used predictive analytics and machine learning to develop products and solutions to serve Aetna's customers.

Kaity's work is data driven, but she knows that achieving results is not all about the numbers. She is on a mission to make a positive impact on public health. In college, she planned to be a doctor. But the more she learned about the health care system, the more she realized that she might be of greater service by working in public health rather than in medicine. So she decided to get a master's in public health with a focus on health policy and management.

After graduation, she joined Aetna (which was later acquired by CVS) and was soon tasked with a project to make saving and paying for health care simple. Her job was to manage a team rolling out a product that would give patients an option to pay for their health care inside the CVS app. Ideally, this service would simplify bill payment, benefiting the company and their customers.

The rollout seemed to go well, and the development team was eager to move on to designing more features for the product. Although that group gave the customer service team the job of responding to questions or feedback, Kaity would routinely scroll through customers' messages. Most were straightforward. People couldn't find the payment button, for example, and just needed basic guidance about the process. However, the messages from one man stood out. He repeatedly contacted the company with complaints about the payment mechanism. He said he was getting charged for duplicate payments and not getting credit for payments he had made. He was infuriated that he was getting notices that his payments were overdue, and he was starting to receive calls from collection agencies.

He seemed like an outlier to the customer service team, who chalked up his problems to his lack of tech savvy rather than a glitch in the product.

Kaity persisted, however, in learning more. "Let's just talk to this guy," she urged her team. She got two data engineers to join her on a Zoom call with the customer so they could ask him to share his screen to understand what he was seeing. Sure enough, what he revealed was a major software issue. Somehow the program allowed duplicate payments and did not reconcile them in the system. On the company's end, it appeared that the payments had not been received. The team fixed the problem quickly, and they now routinely invite this user to beta-test other applications.

Eventually, the data team would have realized the problem and gotten it fixed without this session with a frustrated customer. However, the Zoom call sped up the process and served the customer well.

Listening Creates Deeper Connections

Susie Nam is a recognized leader in the demanding world of advertising. Most recently she was CEO for the Americas at Droga5, a global, award-winning advertising agency whose clients range from JPMorgan Chase to Huggies. Under her watch, the agency grew from a staff of 35 to a team of 650 with offices in the U.S., U.K., Brazil, and Japan.

Susie brings a passion for achieving greater diversity and inclusion across the industry. Since 2017 she has been on the board (and is now chair) of ADCOLOR, an organization that champions diversity and inclusion in the creative industry—helping people "rise up" to be recognized for their work and to "reach back" to help others shine.

While at Droga5, she was determined to develop programs that built interracial relationships that advanced talent who were Black,

Indigenous, and people of color (BIPOC) and created more authentic storytelling in advertising. Listening was a critical part of this effort.

She laughed when I asked her if listening was just a part of being an expert marketing/advertising professional. "Actually, we are bred to be show horses," she told me. "We are bred to persuade, to have a point of view, to have comprehensively substantiated ideas that feel neat and distinctive and breakthrough. Then we try to make these ideas bulletproof. That's what we do. It's not to say we don't listen—especially in early stages of development. We listen to get to the insight and the strategy and the jumping-off point for the creative, but once we have our idea, I'm not sure we are super-great listeners. And we celebrate those who get things over the line."

So her focus on listening to achieve culture change at Droga5 may have felt like a fresh and bold approach to some of her colleagues. When she launched a pilot to explore ways to enhance diversity and inclusion in the firm, she convened 10 people—five BIPOC and five white—from across the agency. Each agreed to participate in a six-week program to get to know each other better.

Each week, participants met in pairs to listen to each other as they answered questions that explored different stages of their lives, their upbringing, and their relationship with work. Among the questions: What was your first job? Did you have to work? What did you do with the first dollar you made? What does success look like for you?

All 10 participants also met as a group each Friday to discuss what they had learned from the paired conversations. Susie introduced various exercises and speakers to challenge the group further.

This six-week process was unforgettable for those who took part, and it delivered results. "They gave me a slew of ideas," Susie reported, "and each one agreed to be part of a kickoff session for the subsequent pilot. They were so generous, really invested in moving the work forward."

Developing Listening Mastery

Listening is simple and effective. So why don't we do more of it? For starters, many of us don't understand how critical it is to our success.

Second, we assume that we know how to listen—no practice required. That is not the case.

Fortunately, learning how to be a better listener isn't like weight training. You don't have to put in months of effort, but you do have to commit to engaging differently with others, and you must break some habits.

▶ ASSESS YOUR LISTENING COMPETENCE

To write her book *You're Not Listening: What You're Missing and Why It Matters*, Kate Murphy conducted hundreds of interviews. She routinely asked her interviewees, "Who listens to you?" Almost always the question was greeted with a pause. She said that the lucky ones could come up with a couple of people, but many said that nobody in their lives really listened to them.[6]

These findings suggest to me that one step in becoming a better listener is to think about your own circle of close friends and relatives and assess how much listening is actually happening.

You can begin by identifying up to five people in that circle who are very close to you. Write down their names. Then, using a score of 1 to 5, assess each person as a listener. A score of 1 means that they never listen and frequently interrupt. A score of 5 means that this person always takes time to hear what you have to say without judging or interrupting or telling you what they think.

Reflect on your responses. Which person in this group do you think is the best listener? Why? In what ways would you say your life is enriched by having someone in your circle who listens so attentively?

Then reverse the scoring. Ask yourself how you think these five people would respond if they were asked (anonymously) to assess your listening skill. Use the same 1 to 5 scale. Would they say they can usually count on you to listen attentively to them?

Are you happy with the score you assigned to yourself? If not, think about where you would like to score on that continuum. If your imagined score falls below that number, challenge yourself by asking, "What might be possible in these relationships if I were to make a concerted effort to be a more effective listener?" Then ask, "What am I willing to commit to do to increase my score?"

If you believe there is a pathway to deeper relationships as a result of becoming a more gifted listener, you'll be more likely to do what it takes to make a change.

▶ WHEN LISTENING, ENDEAVOR TO MAKE OTHERS FEEL HEARD

In all of my reading and thinking about listening, the most profound insight I have discovered comes from Maya Angelou, American author and winner of the Presidential Medal of Freedom, who famously said, "I've learned that people will forget what you said, people will forget what you did, but people will never forget how you made them feel." Whether and how you listen to someone matters enormously with regard to how they feel about themselves and about you—and, importantly, about the new idea you espouse.

Why can listening have such a profound effect?

Stephen Covey, the renowned efficiency expert, says that when you really listen to another person with the intent first to understand, then to be understood, "it's like giving them psychological air."[7] Henri Nouwen, a Dutch philosopher, refers to listening as "a form of spiritual hospitality."[8]

Susie Nam's pilot demonstrated to all participants the power of being heard. Susie recalled the impact on her personally. "I came into this initiative with an intent to listen and inquire actively. I wanted to engage with a level of discourse I thought would be needed for someone to really get to know me. In the pilot there were people I had known for over 10 years and others who had been at the firm a much shorter time. What I found really astounding was that as I listened intently, everyone felt new to me. I was surprised to learn that I had really known nothing about each person—even if we had worked closely together for years. The experience changed me permanently in a lot of ways. Going forward, whether I am working with a colleague or clients, I will bring a lot more curiosity about them. I believe others who participated will do the same."

▶ PUT AWAY THE ELECTRONICS

We can't hear each other if we let electronics distract us.

There is not one of us who has not been in a conversation that we thought was really important when the person listening glanced at their phone or, with a quick apology, answered a call, with an aside, "Sorry. I've got to get this. It will just take a minute." Maybe it does take just a minute, but the mood has shifted. The chain of thought has been disrupted, and it is a rare pair of interlocutors who can get back to where they were without effort.

We know that the rule about putting the electronics away is important, but we violate it daily simply by keeping our phones in plain sight.

It turns out that even the sight of a phone detracts from meaningful communication. Sherry Turkle, an MIT professor who conducts research on the social and psychological effects of technology, points out, "Studies of conversations both in the laboratory and in natural settings show that when two people are talking, the mere presence of a phone on a table between them or in the periphery of their vision changes both what they talk about and the degree of connection they feel. People keep the conversation on topics where they won't mind being interrupted. They don't feel as invested in each other. Even a silent phone disconnects us."[9]

▶ PAY ATTENTION, BE INTERESTED, AND DON'T INTERRUPT

For most of us, interrupting is a habit that is very hard to break. We justify interruptions in multiple ways. We seek clarification on someone's point. Or we want to correct them before they say something we "know" is going to be wrong. Or we want to offer our agreement. Or we act as if their unfinished comment inspired a thought that we just have to make right then. Because the interruptions seem completely appropriate to us, we don't even realize how often we cut people off mid-sentence.

Stephen Covey explains that when we listen and interrupt in this way, we are bringing our own autobiography into the conversation, and that makes it impossible for us to listen empathetically.[10]

Only by becoming aware of these habits can we begin to make a change.

If you need to be convinced that interrupting is a common disruptive practice in your discourse, try keeping count for one week of how often you are interrupted and how often you interrupt. I guarantee that you will be surprised at the results.

▶ PRACTICE LISTENING

In the seminars with First Movers, we use a 10-minute exercise to give Fellows a chance to practice listening. First, we read a short poem.

An excellent poem for this exercise is "The Good Life," by Tracy K. Smith, from her Pulitzer Prize–winning poetry collection, *Life on Mars*.

> When some people talk about money
> They speak as if it were a mysterious lover
> Who went out to buy milk and never
> Came back, and it makes me nostalgic
> For the years I lived on coffee and bread,
> Hungry all the time, walking to work on payday
> Like a woman journeying for water
> From a village without a well, then living
> One or two nights like everyone else
> On roast chicken and red wine.

After reading the poem, we ask the Fellows to pair up. They take turns being the speaker and the listener. Each speaker has three minutes to answer some reflection questions, such as: How do you define the good life for yourself? How has your definition of the good life changed over the years? Who in your life serves as a model for "the good life" as you define it?

When the speaker is talking, the listener must stay silent and simply listen to the speaker. If the speaker runs out of things to say, both are told to sit quietly until it is time to reverse roles.

After each person has had a turn to speak and to listen, they are invited to debrief in their pairs for four minutes. Questions for the debrief include: What did it feel like to be listened to? What did it feel like to listen?

Fellows report that the exercise feels uncomfortable but liberating. They are surprised to realize how much they can hear and communicate in just three minutes of attentive listening and speaking. They also realize that by not introducing their own "autobiography," they allow those who are speaking to choose their own route in the conversation.

▶ ALLOW FOR SILENCE

As the above exercise is designed to show, when you learn to listen, you realize that you don't need to fill every minute with words. Pausing in a conversation gives others a chance to collect their thoughts, and it leaves an opening for others to express themselves.

Becoming comfortable with silence is one of the most important things I have learned as a dialogue facilitator. Early on, I thought that my role was to keep the conversation going. If I posed a question to the group and no one responded immediately, I would restate the question or provide additional commentary. But I have learned that people will ask for clarification if they need it. Silence generally means something else. People are thinking or giving others a chance to get their voice into the conversation.

Allowing for silence takes practice. I was really uncomfortable the first couple of times I let silence hang in the room. When the conversation pauses, 10 seconds can feel like an eternity. But with years of practice, I now know the benefit of waiting more than a few beats for someone to speak.

▶ MODEL LISTENING

At the end of First Movers seminars, we ask Fellows to complete an evaluation and let us know how the program has impacted them personally. With almost every class, over 50 percent of the Fellows report that they have become better listeners. Often that response is 70 percent or higher.

This response may be explained in part by the fact that during the year of seminars, we include a session that focuses on the importance of listening and highlights strategies for doing it better. I run that session, so I would like to claim a personal victory for these scores.

However, I think what really enhances participants' listening ability is the way we structure group conversations. My colleague Eli Malinsky, who directed the Fellowship Program for several years, puts it this way: "In the seminar setting we create, each person realizes that their job is to be one of 20 voices. The format of the seminar itself demands 'turn taking.' When one person speaks, the others listen. And we don't allow phones on the table."

By making time for shared conversation, we also see that participants begin to reference or build on—rather than talk over—points made by others. The environment itself sets an expectation for engagement and attentive listening that quickly spreads through the group.

Listening, it seems, is contagious. If you model listening by your own behavior and by the context you create, you encourage others to follow your lead.

Henry David Thoreau, the 19th-century American naturalist and philosopher, wrote, "The greatest compliment that was ever paid me was when one asked me what I thought, and attended to my answer."[11] When you extend to others the courtesy of listening to them, they are likely to return the favor.

SECTION 4

Staying on Course

*Only those who risk going too far
can find out how far they can go.*

—T. S. ELIOT, PREFACE, *TRANSIT OF VENUS: POEMS,*
BY HARRY CROSBY

CHAPTER 10

Dare to Step Up

L ike other classmates in his MBA program at Yale, Anupam Bhargava sought the best possible job after graduation. He was a very attractive candidate for the companies that recruited on campus. He had an undergraduate degree in mechanical engineering, had experience as a consultant, and was the kind of outgoing and personable colleague whom everyone would want on a team. Jobs in consulting, venture capital, and finance were the preferred options for graduates with his profile, and those options were certainly available to Anupam.

He made a different choice. To the surprise of his friends, Anupam accepted an offer to join the leadership program at United Technologies Corporation (UTC). It was a decision that seemed best aligned with his commitment to use his training in engineering and business to address environmental and social challenges. With that choice, he became one of two graduates in his class who went directly into industry—passing up more lucrative opportunities in both venture capital and private equity.

Rapidly he demonstrated his value to the company and was offered a newly created position as an analyst for the storied CEO and chairman, George David. Anupam would be a content expert in areas that he cared deeply about, such as global warming.

His managers urged him to accept this prestigious position. Nevertheless, he declined. He elected instead to help form an incubator within Pratt & Whitney, a UTC subsidiary. It was a new profit and loss division with a specific mission: to commercialize clean technology. "The role wasn't prestigious at all because the venture was an unknown," Anupam explained. "I was the first employee, and there was no defined path."

Anupam dared to accept this assignment because it positioned him to be on the front lines of change. He knew that it was a leap, but he was keen to figure out how to build this business.

The risks were real, but the scale of the opportunity was massive. For example, Pratt & Whitney, one of the top three jet engine manufacturers in the world, had been asked to solve a problem posed by a customer, one of the world's largest airlines: "Help us improve jet engine health while the engine is still on the aircraft." The request might sound simple, but as Anupam explained, it was revolutionary.

"What Pratt & Whitney had done for years was to build engines, sell them, build spare parts, sell them. And then we became a service provider. Customers sent us their engines, and we would overhaul them. What we'd never done in our 90-plus years of history was actually take our business to the workplace of our customer, which, in the case of our airline customers, was at airports around the world."

If Anupam could find a way to take engine repair to the airports, aircraft worldwide could be serviced on-site, saving millions of gallons of fuel and reducing carbon dioxide emissions. Yet again he heard the voices around him: "It hasn't been done. You won't be able to do it. This is too big of a problem to tackle." But as Anupam said, "That, of course, made me want to do it more."

As he recalled, "We didn't have an infrastructure to support what we were trying to do. So when we were planning to work on our first airplanes at JFK overnight when aircraft were parked at the gate, we had to borrow trucks, rent generators, beg for hangar space at the airport, and moonlight on our day jobs to execute the pilot. We were as much of a start-up as you can imagine. The fact that I was running the enterprise didn't matter; I was also the truck driver and the floor sweeper."

To make matters even more challenging, they launched this service in airports in the midst of the heightened security put in place in the wake of the September 11, 2001, terrorist attacks. Nonetheless, Anupam and his devoted team kept at it and succeeded. They partnered with a small technology company and leveraged the tremendous engineering capabilities of Pratt & Whitney to find a solution that worked. But it was the scrappiness and fierce determination of the team that made this idea a reality.

"One of the really cool things that happened," he remembered, "and why I knew I made the right choice, was that when I began working on this initiative, talented people started to come out of the woodwork who were eager to join the team. These amazing people helped us build what became an industry-changing business."

I love Anupam's story and the joy I hear when he tells it. The EcoPower Services business he launched at Pratt & Whitney has now serviced tens of thousands of engines on aircraft around the world. And the environmental benefits have been proved. Because the process reduces fuel burn, it lowers carbon dioxide emissions and has saved millions of gallons of fuel and the corresponding CO_2 emissions. Importantly, this innovation has become a best practice for the aviation industry. And the environmental benefits have been scaled globally.

Anupam has gone on to make more surprising career moves. Several years ago, he and his family packed up their Connecticut home and moved to Denmark, where Anupam took on a leadership role at Grundfos, a company that develops water solutions for the world. More recently, he became executive vice president and head of innovation, service, and customer experience at another Danish company, Nilfisk, a worldwide leader in professional cleaning products and services.

To help him make professional choices throughout his career, even when they have seemed unconventional or gone against solid advice, Anupam has used what he calls an "impact compass," which he described in a LinkedIn post several years ago as "the aligning force behind a purpose driven career where an individual makes conscious decisions on where (and where not) to apply their professional efforts."[1]

Anupam referred to this compass as being an "internal driver" that might cause you, for example, to pass up a big promotion in favor of another option that at first may appear to be a step backward but over the long term aligns more closely with your values and the impact you want to achieve in your career.

In his case, his compass has guided him to pursue a career that is rooted in his intent to create positive social and environmental impact within whatever industry he is working in.

Acting Boldly When You Know What's Right

Anupam is also an advocate for Giving Voice to Values (GVV),[2] an approach for preparing individuals to speak up and take chances and to act on the values they prize. It was created by Mary Gentile, who has served on the First Movers design and facilitation team since the program's inception.

GVV, now an established component in the First Movers program, is an innovative curriculum for developing the skills, knowledge, and commitment required to implement values-based leadership. It is taught in organizations around the world. Unlike many programs that teach ethical decision-making, GVV doesn't focus on helping people figure out what is right and wrong. Rather, it provides essential tools that enable people to act effectively when they already know the right thing to do.

During the seminars with Fellows, we hear many examples of intrapreneurs who have acted on their values—even when it was hard and risky. These stories inspire others to do the same.

Jenifer Bice, for example, was director of global associate communications at Walmart when she was asked to travel to China to work with a human resources team on a reorganization initiative. At the time, she was managing internal communications with Walmart employees (called "associates"). Her job was to enhance associates' experience and engage with employees at all levels. Although she was based in Arkansas, Jenifer had made several international trips, including to China, to do research that would help the company better engage with local employees there.

The new assignment came in the wake of Walmart's decision to consolidate about 18 separate purchasing offices throughout China down to three. The move would change the jobs and even job locations of many workers. Although she did not have deep expertise in that market, she had done change management before and felt equipped to assist in this effort.

When she arrived, however, she learned that the change was more complex than she had thought. Some years earlier, a much smaller reorganization had led to significant labor unrest, greatly challenging the company in this important market. It was clear to her that they had to find a different way of managing this process to deliver positive outcomes for the employees and the communities in which they lived and worked.

She was told the senior management team wanted to retain as many employees as possible in the move. So she was surprised to learn that her colleagues in human resources were not preparing for any retentions. Because of cultural and economic factors unique to China, they believed the moves would be too disruptive for employees and their families and that associates would opt for the severance package. As one colleague told Jenifer, "If anyone stays, the number will be very small, so I'm not worried about that."

Jenifer had been sent to play a supporting role in a change management process that was already in place. But she realized that she would need to step up and lead in developing the change management and communications plan. So she responded emphatically, "Well, we need to worry about it. We can't tell employees we want them to stay, that we have jobs for them in other locations, and then when they go to talk to HR, the representative says, 'We didn't think you would do it, so I don't know what to do.'" Jenifer knew that the risk of that exchange was a disenfranchised employee.

Realizing the need for a coordinated approach, Jenifer brought various staff involved in the change management endeavor into closer alignment and pushed them to be more intentional about serving the needs of the associates affected by the consolidation.

For five weeks, she and the team back in the U.S. worked 24 hours a day to get ready for the change. She would put in a full day in China and then pass off the work to her colleagues in the U.S. They developed tools and resources for HR and associates, including a Q&A sheet in Mandarin. They did scenario planning, preparing for contingencies. Also, they started working with the government relations team in China. They wanted to be sure that messages and timing were aligned across the business leaders, HR, the communications team, and the government relations experts.

When the consolidation was announced, they were ready. In the end, 40 percent of associates elected to stay with Walmart. Over the months that followed, the business benefits of the consolidation plan became evident, and the change was accomplished without any labor disruption or negative press.

As Jenifer recounted this story to me, I recalled an earlier conversation we'd had. She told me about cheerleading from high school through college, followed by years of coaching cheerleading squads. I asked her whether that experience influenced the way she had responded to the challenge in China.

"Yes," she said, "I think it gave me gumption."

She recalled the stress of trying out for a cheerleading squad, performing in front of thousands of people, and standing in a crowded arena trying to sell calendars to raise money to buy team uniforms. "Later, when I was coaching little kids, I remember doing media interviews on behalf of the team," she said. "In that moment, you had to pull it together and figure it out."

Even more important, she reflected, her cheerleading experience helped her develop a deep commitment to helping others. "I have told my team at work that 'I'm here to offer you whatever support you need.'" That training and determination stood her in good stead as she worked closely with her human resources colleagues to deliver a smooth organizational transition in China.

Dave Gallon, another Fellow, shared a very different story of challenging organizational norms. One day he decided to wear jeans and sneakers to work.

Dave joined Toyota in the U.S. in 2002 and enjoyed his initial assignments working for a company that cared about the impact it was making on the environment and communities.

Over the years, however, he started to feel that the company was becoming more risk-averse and was doing less to create space that was truly authentic for employees. Therefore, he eagerly accepted an opportunity to work with a vice president he admired who invited him to find ways to "make Toyota more like a place where you would want to work."

He did research at innovative companies to understand the processes they had put in place to build creative environments. He quickly realized, "It's not a process; it's the culture. People weren't creating innovation, they were living it."

At one point, he visited Zappos in Las Vegas and met its legendary founder and CEO, the late Tony Hsieh. Sitting in one of Zappos's conference rooms, Dave looked out at the staff. "How do you start this transformation?" he asked. Hsieh's answer was unexpected: "Well, first thing, let people wear what they want to work."

That conversation made him think of other workplaces he had been in where corporate dress codes did not rule. At one established tech company, he went into a meeting with a salesperson in a suit; a business strategist dressed in jeans and a sweater; and a programmer with multiple piercings, a purple mohawk haircut, and ripped jeans. "What they were wearing," Dave observed, "had nothing to do with how they contributed to the effort."

This sartorial display would not have been possible then at Toyota, which had a strict dress code. But a day after that meeting, Dave opened his closet to get ready for work, and he made a fateful decision: "I'm going to wear whatever I want to work." So he donned a pair of jeans and sneakers and set off.

He got away with this transgression for a time, but HR began to take notice. So did colleagues, who asked their bosses if they could wear casual clothes to work too.

By this time, Dave had accumulated research that demonstrated the positive impact on culture that came with relaxing dress codes. He ratcheted up his campaign. He sent an email to all of the group vice presidents in the organization, arguing for a more lenient dress code and attaching his research.

The email got an immediate response. The head of HR summoned him to her office, where she sat with three of her direct reports. It was in the early 2000s, a time of considerable financial and operational stress for Toyota.

Dave stood in front of the group and dared to say, "If you are going to fire me for wearing jeans and sneakers because that's the most important thing you have to do at the moment, I'll put it on the top of my résumé. However, if you want to know why I'm doing it, I'll be glad to explain." They talked for two hours.

Within a short time, Toyota U.S. loosened the dress code, and even top executives began wearing jeans to work. That was a victory in itself, but what this change sparked was even more important. People said to him, "You inspired me by putting something you cared about on the line and getting results. I didn't think the company would do it." The loosening dress code restrictions signaled that other change was possible; and, indeed, this small, symbolic action led to many more substantial changes.

"Toyota has renewed its understanding that you get better business results—better products, the best talent, and better results for society—when you create an organization that is collaborative, coordinated, and creative," Dave told me. Toyota is now on a path to transform from being a manufacturer of world-class vehicles into what it calls a "mobility company," one that serves the mobility needs of its customers to enhance their quality of life, which could mean exploring a range of innovations such as car sharing, self-driving cars, subscription services, electric bikes, and beyond.

Would the change have happened without Dave's act of sartorial insurgency? Probably. But relaxing the dress code may have been a "crossing the Rubicon" moment for the company and accelerated the process.

Learning to Act on Your Values

Anupam's, Jenifer's, and Dave's stories are not anomalies. I see frequent examples of people taking action to support innovative ideas that go against corporate norms. However, I also see hesitancy. Many people aspire to challenge the status quo but aren't quite sure they are the right ones to speak out, or if it's the right time to advocate for change, or if they have the tools to make the case. I understand their caution, of course. All corporate social intrapreneurs face inevitable headwinds that make action difficult—corporate reorganizations, downsizing, dismissive bosses, and the classic organizational mantras: "It's never worked before" and "We don't do that here."

Therefore, one aspect of my work that makes me most proud is when Fellows report that as a result of being in our program, they have greater confidence to champion the changes they want to see in their companies.

To be clear—it's not that they know exactly how to achieve these changes. In fact, if we have done our job in these seminars correctly, the Fellows know that engaging others to design the pathways for achieving the organizational changes they seek is essential. But they have confidence to catalyze a change with a clear end view in sight.

To do so, they must speak up and take chances.

Part of their confidence comes from being in community with others who share their commitment to change. But their study of Giving Voice to Values gives them strategies for speaking up. They also learn an important truth: that developing this capacity can be learned.

The GVV framework is often used to help people develop an approach for speaking up in situations where they are being pressured to act in a way that goes against their personal values. These situations arise repeatedly in all professions and in our daily life, when one can use GVV effectively to say no to a practice that violates our values.

In working with corporate social intrapreneurs, Mary Gentile flips the narrative and uses the GVV framework not to effectively oppose an action but instead to speak affirmatively in favor of a new social innovation, one that may go against long-established norms and practices within their companies.

As Mary explained, "GVV allows us to shift from aiming for moral courage to building moral competence. To do so, we need to practice and prepare. Much like athletes who gain muscle memory through intense practice, corporate social intrapreneurs need to build moral muscle memory."

▶ START WITH A "TALE OF TWO STORIES" EXERCISE

As an introduction to the GVV approach, Mary asks Fellows to complete an exercise she calls the "Tale of Two Stories." The intent is to prompt them to recall times when they felt empowered to voice their values within the workplace and other times when they experienced circumstances that inhibited that action. In small groups, Fellows then share their responses to questions for each story.

Reflecting on when they were able to act on their values, they recount what they did and the impact of their actions. They discuss what motivated them to speak up and act. They report how satisfied they were with their actions and whether there were other ways they wish they had acted. Then they think about the factors that enabled or inhibited them and whether these factors were in their own control or within the control of others.

They answer converse questions for times when they declined to act on their values.

When they have finished, the Fellows consider what they learned from recalling these experiences. Particularly when they were unable to act on their values, they are invited to consider how advance preparation might have led to a different outcome.

Then they consider how they might apply these lessons when "moral competence" would help them overcome a challenge, now or in the future.

You can do this exercise on your own. Or find a partner to join you and then discuss the results.

The "Tale of Two Stories" exercise provides a solid foundation for learning how to give voice to your values and understanding the role that moral competence plays in working effectively as a corporate social intrapreneur. It is also an introduction to the seven pillars of GVV: values; choice; normality; purpose; self-knowledge, self-image, and alignment; voice; reasons and rationalizations.[3] Below are strategies for understanding and activating these pillars.

▶ IDENTIFY YOUR VALUES AND PURPOSE

The foundation for Giving Voice to Values is getting clear on what values you hold most dear—for example, honesty, respect, responsibility. These are the same values that you identified in chapter 2 to help you discover your purpose.

Mary Gentile emphasizes that it's important to know your values and your personal and professional purpose before any values conflicts arise.

Writing down why you do the work you do and the impact that you hope to have will help you gain that clarity.

This knowledge serves as a bulwark in conversations with colleagues. Realizing how meaningful it is for you to know your values and purpose can also prompt you to seek insights about the values and purpose of your colleagues.

To use the GVV strategy to help you drive positive change in your organization, think about the innovation you envision. Then identify which of your values are built into your assumptions about the innovation. Write them down. (Is your idea for a new product driven, for example, by desires to achieve revenue growth for the firm and to meet the needs of an underserved population? Such an idea may signal that you place considerable value on equity and inclusion.)

When you present your idea to others and invite their input, consider what values are implicit or explicit in their responses. Look for opportunities to identify common ground.

In fact, as Mary Gentile points out, researchers have found a core set of values that are common across cultures and time. The list, including integrity, compassion, and fairness, is short, but it provides clues for how to frame values-based positions in ways that can appeal to and connect with others.[4]

▶ REALIZE YOU HAVE CHOICES

It's easy to feel stuck when values conflicts arise. Forces may seem to be arrayed against you, blocking all avenues for action. But as Mary points out, you actually have more choices than you realize. Reflecting on situations you have dealt with in the past can help you see them more clearly.

Think back to the "Tale of Two Stories" exercise. When you were successful in acting on a value that was important to you, consider the particular circumstances you encountered. Write down what you did that enabled your success. Conversely, in a time when you did not act on your values, or tried to do so without success, recall the circumstances and what factors inhibited your ability to act on your values.

Studying the enablers and inhibitors you have faced provides many clues for what steps to take if you decide to act. Enablers, for example, might include having a supportive boss who listened to your point of view or having a colleague or friend who would support your decision. Another enabler might be your deep conviction that if you choose not to act, you will have to live with the consequences, which might include lasting regret that you didn't try to make a difference.

As you think of what inhibited your action, you may realize, for example, that you felt constrained by time. Or a close friend or colleague, whom you admire, opposed the action. Or a recent corporate reorganization was causing everyone to put their attention elsewhere. One choice you can make is to anticipate the inhibitors, which gives you time to prepare to confront them. Another is to recall ways you have previously defused an inhibitor. You can also seek out an enabler that has worked for you in the past.

▶ SEE VALUES CONFLICTS AS A NORMAL PART OF BUSINESS

Values conflicts are normal in all organizations. Once you recognize that fact, you are less likely to be blindsided when you face one yourself. You are also less likely to think that if you just get through this one conflict, then it will be smooth sailing.

Reflect on the preceding month in your company. Make a list of as many instances as you can recall when people expressed differing points of view. Consider what this list tells you about how often conflicts—large and small—arise in the workplace. You will see that developing strategies for dealing with these conflicts can enhance your performance over the long term—not just help you get through one challenging situation.

Anticipating differences of opinion or expressions of values also lowers the likelihood that you will be triggered emotionally in these circumstances. You will see that they require the same strategic thinking you bring to other aspects of your work.

▶ KNOW YOURSELF AND YOUR STYLE OF ENGAGING

Many of us have preconceived notions about what kinds of people can effectively speak up and act on their values. Those judgments can make us feel that we don't have what it takes to do it. Mary Gentile shows, however, that everyone can find a pathway for speaking up that is consistent with their style. It doesn't matter whether you are an introvert or an extrovert, a risk taker or risk-averse. Her research shows that these traits don't affect the ability of people to act on their values. What distinguishes those who are more effective than others? They have a strong sense of who they are, what capabilities they have, and how they can play to their strengths as they act.

For example, someone adept at responding quickly in situations and at articulating ideas spontaneously may choose to engage one-on-one in conversations. Another who needs time to think through a position may opt for a written memo. You can also bolster your effort by finding others, whose strengths differ from but complement your own, to help make the case.

The important thing is to know yourself and the style of engagement that works best for you. When faced with the need to speak up about your values, think about how to make your case in a manner that is consistent with what you know about yourself and how you want to be perceived by colleagues.

▶ FIND YOUR OWN VOICE—AND PRACTICE USING IT

You will be much more effective in acting on your values if you have practiced voicing them. Think in advance about the points you want to make, and rehearse what you want to say. Imagine various scenarios and how to make the strongest case in each. And then say it out loud.

Practice gives you confidence and allows you to try out ideas and refine how you want to communicate them. Practicing your script in front of others who are willing to give you constructive feedback makes you even better prepared.

If you try speaking up in stress-free situations, you will be better prepared to do so when the situation is more dynamic.

▶ STUDY THE REASONS AND RATIONALIZATIONS GIVEN BY THOSE WHO OPPOSE YOUR IDEA

Anticipating the pushback you are likely to encounter when you try to act on your values gives you the opportunity to script targeted responses. When you are making the case for doing something different in the company, the arguments against the change are often predictable: Implementing the idea will take too much time. It's too complicated. It goes against established practice. The cost will adversely affect quarterly results. We've just been through a recent reorganization, so we can't make this change until things settle down. Etc.

Making a list of all the reasons and rationalizations others might use to block your approach will help you practice responses to deflect them. Using the strategies already presented in this book can also help.

For example, showing how an idea for change aligns with a corporate objective, metric, or founding myth, as we saw in chapter 4, can provide ballast for your argument. Countering resistance by suggesting a low-risk pilot, as described in chapter 5, can lead to a small win that builds momentum for change.

Telling a powerful story about someone whose life might be transformed by your approach, as we saw in chapter 6, can help others see possibilities for change instead of responding negatively to the approach by citing all the reasons why it won't work.

As shown in chapter 7, engaging with others to address an issue elicits a very different response than if you lead with your point of view. Inquiring with carefully crafted questions and listening carefully to responses, as described in chapters 8 and 9, can help you understand reasons and rationalizations.

▶ PRACTICE "CREATIVE COURAGE"

Learning to dare, to give voice to your values and speak up for an idea that matters to you, allows you to practice what Shelly Francis calls "creative courage." In *The Courage Way: Leading and Living with Integrity*, she writes that creative courage may be the type of courage least recognized but the most important for us to cultivate. "It's the courage to come up with creative solutions, to create community, to create meaning from challenges, to create new visions and symbols that other people can rally around, and to create the change that moves us forward in our humanity."[5]

This is the kind of innovative change that First Movers champion. I find it reassuring that we don't have to be born to boldness. We can cultivate it. Mary Gentile's work gives us strategies for building our moral competence in ways that elevate our consciousness and possibilities for action.

*It's only by having some distance
from the world that you can see it whole,
and understand what you should
be doing with it.*

—PICO IYER, "THE JOY OF QUIET," *NEW YORK TIMES*

CHAPTER 11

Reflect Routinely on Purpose

The 19th-century American philosopher and essayist Ralph Waldo Emerson was reputed to have asked friends he encountered after some absence, "What has become clear to you since we last met?" Borrowing from Emerson, we often open morning sessions of First Movers seminars by asking, "What has become clearer to you overnight?"

There is often silence for a few minutes as people think about the previous day. They recall the conversations they had, the insights they gained, and the questions they are now asking.

That simple act of pausing before we move on with our agenda for the day opens a window for all to contribute, and a rich discussion ensues. It demonstrates to everyone what wisdom can be unlocked if we pause and reflect.

Reflection is such a critical practice for anyone trying to make positive change in their company that we view it as one of the four pillars of the First Movers Fellowship Program, along with leadership, innovation, and community.

What Is Reflection?

Tchiki Davis, founder of the Berkeley Well-Being Institute, defines *reflection* as "a mental process you can use to grow your understanding of who you are, what your values are, and why you think, feel, and act the way you do. When you self-reflect and become more conscious of what drives you," she notes, "you can more easily make changes that help you more easily develop your self or improve your life."[1]

Howard Gardner, a psychologist and professor known for his work on multiple intelligences, writes that reflection is "regular, conscious consideration of the events of daily life, in the light of long-term aspirations." It is a deliberate act that, according to Gardner, becomes even more critical as we age. "Having reached our adult years, and attained a certain level of competence in our chosen pursuits," Gardner explains, "we cannot assume that lessons from experience will automatically dawn on us." Reflecting, he continues, gives us the opportunity to understand "what has happened to us and what it means—what we are trying to achieve and whether we have succeeded."[2]

As a student, teacher, parent, even a banker, over many years I had glimpsed the power of reflection. However, it wasn't until I came to the Aspen Institute that I began to understand more deeply the central role that reflection plays in enhancing our ability to live a rewarding personal and professional life, one rooted in meaning and purpose.

Reflection has been at the center of programming at the Aspen Institute since its founding in 1950 by Walter Paepcke, then CEO of the Container Corporation. Paepcke had taken the Great Books seminar at the University of Chicago facilitated by the philosopher Mortimer Adler. It inspired him to envision a seminar program, to be held in Aspen, Colorado, in which business leaders (whom he notoriously referred to as "the great unwashed") could come together to read and discuss selections from works of classic and modern writers. Using these texts as the foundation for dialogue, "seminarians," as they were called, would wrestle with challenging questions that arise when we seek to reconcile the tensions that underpin the fundamental ideas of economic, social, and political systems: liberty, equality, community, efficiency.[3]

Paepcke was explicit about the goal of this program. "The Executive Seminar was not intended to make a corporate treasurer a more skilled corporate treasurer, but to help a leader gain access to his or her own humanity by becoming more self-aware, more self-correcting, and more self-fulfilling."[4]

As we help Fellows build the courage and capacity to be effective change agents in their companies, we too hope that offering opportunities to reflect will help them become more self-aware, self-correcting, and self-fulfilling. And with each class of Fellows, that hope appears to be realized. Fellows often cite the emphasis on reflection as one of the most transformative aspects of the program for them. They see that they have not been taking enough time to step back from the press of their daily responsibilities to consider their lives in a broader context and that it is up to them to make a conscious choice to do so.

We Want to Reflect. Why Don't We Do It?

In the Fellowship Program, we ask Fellows to complete a Leadership Reflection Guide so they can identify the strengths they bring to their roles as change agents and to uncover areas where they could develop further. Across all cohorts, one finding is consistent: Fellows report that they fall short on taking time to reflect, and they want to do better.

Several reasons explain why there is such a disconnect between aspirations and action.

For one thing, although Fellows think they should be more reflective, they aren't really sure why. They don't see a clear line from reflection to well-being, performance, and a purpose-driven life. Jennifer Porter, a leadership coach, draws that line. "Reflection," she writes, gives the brain an opportunity to pause amidst the chaos, untangle and sort through observations and experiences, consider multiple possible interpretations, and create meaning. This meaning becomes learning which can then inform future mindsets and actions."[5]

As Fellows are exposed to more opportunities to reflect, they come to realize that it delivers multiple benefits. It increases their self-awareness so they can show up more authentically at home and at work. It helps them discover and stay in touch with their personal purpose and to connect that purpose to their professional endeavors. Reflection also helps them consider their decisions across time and in the context of their greater aspirations so they can move forward with greater confidence and conviction.

A second inhibitor is that people see reflection as a luxury, not a necessity. One Fellow told me that with all of her responsibilities at work and to her family, taking time for herself to reflect seemed like a peripheral and self-interested activity that she could easily give up. When she realized the importance of reflection for helping her become a better professional and parent, she no longer saw the practice as an "add-on" but rather as a critical step on the path toward living her best life.

A third inhibitor is that we are ensnared by busyness. Making reflection a priority requires giving up busyness as a badge of honor—or, as Tim Kreider, cartoonist and essayist, more darkly calls it, a "kind of existential reassurance, a hedge against emptiness."[6]

In seminars with Fellows, Dave Sluyter, a member of the First Movers design team and former CEO of the Fetzer Institute, points out how often we respond to friends' casual "How are you?" inquiries by saying we are "so busy." What, he asks, if we were to respond instead by saying, "Great. I'm leading a rich and fulfilling life." How would that change our internal narrative about how we spend our days?

Being too busy to make space for reflection is not simply a modern-day phenomenon. Years ago, Dorothy Canfield Fisher, a 20th-century American reformer and author, quipped, "If we would only give, just once, the same amount of reflection to what we want to get out of life that we give to the question of what to do with a two weeks' vacation, we would be startled by our false standards and the aimless procession of our busy days."

Fisher's critique is brutal, but it serves as a startling reminder that de-prioritizing reflection comes at a personal cost.

Finally, a significant barrier for many people who seek to reflect is that they don't know how to do it. It feels like a kind of mystical practice that is out of reach for them. That is far from the truth.

Tips for Incorporating Reflection into Your Life

The rest of this chapter offers suggestions for jump-starting your reflection practice and incorporating introspection into your life. Hopefully, they will demonstrate that there are many ways to become more reflective; and while the result can be transformative, it isn't necessary to make major changes in your life in order to benefit.

▶ START SMALL

Reflection doesn't require a seven-day silent retreat.

When you seek to establish any new habit, it's useful to think about making one small change rather than attempting a fundamental redesign of your schedule.

Over the years, we have heard Fellows say that they intend to set aside, say, an hour three times a week to reflect. Or they plan to keep Saturday morning free for reflection. Then the urgency of the day presses in, and that time gets reallocated.

You are more likely to succeed if you set a small, very specific goal. Neil Pasricha, author of *The Happiness Equation*, recommends starting the day with a two-minute exercise. Every day, he writes his responses to three prompts: I will let go of . . . I am grateful for . . . I will focus on . . . .[7]

Choose what works for you, but be precise and constrained. As an example, try setting a goal of taking 15 minutes twice a week for one month at noon on Wednesdays and Fridays. Put the times on your calendar. As the month draws to a close, ask what you have learned in the process and decide what your goal will be for the month to come.

▶ TAKE A BREATH

In the spirit of starting small, try taking a single breath. Thich Nhat Hanh, a Vietnamese monk known to some as the father of mindfulness, assures us, "Anyone can succeed in the practice of a single conscious breath. If we continue to breathe consciously for ten breaths, without our mind going astray, then we have taken a valuable step on the path of practice. If we can practice conscious breathing for ten minutes, an important change will take place in us."[8]

We often start sessions with Fellows by inviting them to take several deep breaths. We found this practice especially helpful during those long months as the pandemic raged when all of us were on continuous Zoom calls. Before diving into our agendas, we suggested that people turn off their video, close their eyes, and take several conscious breaths. It gave them a chance to center themselves and make a transition from whatever they had been doing before joining us online. It works at the end of a call as well.

▶ DEVELOP YOUR OWN REFLECTION QUESTIONS

Not knowing what to do when you reflect is an inhibitor for many. People set aside time to think or pull out their journals and then find themselves staring helplessly into space or at a blank page.

Getting clear on the questions that will spark your reflection makes it much easier to begin. As Judy Brown writes in *A Leader's Guide to Reflective Practice*, "Perhaps the greatest resource for reflection is the power of a good question, one which places us in a genuinely open and curious mind-set, and invites further exploration of what is going on."[9] She offers many provocative thought starters in her invaluable guide, including: What is the limit I'd most like to break through? What am I noticing? What is surprising me?

Paying attention to the kinds of questions that experienced leadership coaches ask their clients can give you many ideas for questions you can incorporate into your own reflection practice.

Marshall Goldsmith, a renowned leadership coach, believes that it's important to ask yourself six "active" questions every day. Each begins the same way: "Did I do my best to . . . increase my happiness . . . find meaning . . . be engaged . . . build positive relationships . . . set clear goals . . . make progress toward goal achievement?"[10]

Muriel Wilkins's *Coaching Real Leaders* podcast gives an inside look into the leadership coaching process with one of today's gifted leadership coaches. In her sessions with people facing leadership challenges, she often asks plenty of questions that could work for you as well. They include: What does success look like for you? How does your team perceive you? What are you telling yourself about your own performance and about how you show up at work? Is this narrative serving you? Can you shift your inner dialogue?[11]

When you set an intention to look for questions to ground your reflection practice, you will begin to see them everywhere. Make note of them, and decide which ones work best for you.

▶ FIND A REFLECTION PRACTICE THAT WORKS FOR YOU

There is no single key to unlock the power of reflection in our own lives. The important thing is to find a consistent practice, or several practices, that you commit to do and to give yourself time to think by moving away, however briefly, from your compulsion to act.

In his practical guide to reflection, *Step Back: How to Bring the Art of Reflection into Your Busy Life,* Joseph Badaracco, a professor of business ethics, proposes thinking about reflection as a mosaic, an artful collection of practices that can fit into "the cracks and crevices of . . . everyday lives." To build this mosaic, he suggests keeping four essential design principles in mind, which he explores in separate chapters of his book. The first is to "aim for good enough," not for some ideal of reflection perfection. Second is to "downshift occasionally" in order to "suspend your default mental habits of analytical thinking, cost-benefit analysis, and planning next steps." The next is to "ponder the tough issues" with an emphasis on the importance of pondering, which, Badaracco explains, is "trying to grasp what really matters about an issue or a problem by coming back to it again and again and looking at it from a variety of angles." And, finally, he recommends that we "pause and measure up" to consider how best to meet the standards that others expect of us and that we expect of ourselves.[12]

▶ USE MILESTONES THROUGHOUT THE YEAR AS REFLECTION PROMPTS

Birthdays, anniversaries, the winter and summer solstices, and the arrival of a new year offer excellent, recurring prompts to pause and reflect.

Anticipating a new year, with so much talk about resolutions, is a particularly fruitful time for reflection. For several years, we have hosted discussions with Fellows to learn about the reflection practices they have established. Their activities are wide ranging. One Fellow, for example, routinely goes on a retreat at the end of the year to bike, read, and spend time with family. Other Fellows scrutinize their calendars over the past 12 months so they can better understand the themes, activities, and people that featured prominently throughout the year. Using that knowledge, they can then choose whether to build on or change these aspects of their lives in the year to come. Others set aside time with partners and children to review their photos from the year, select their favorites, and create a printed photo book that tells their collective story of the moments that mattered most to them and the memories they want to preserve.

These activities are diverse, but there is a common thread. Each is an intentional effort to take advantage of a special moment in the year to pause and move more thoughtfully into the future.

▶ **CULTIVATE MINDFULNESS**

There is growing public awareness that developing mindfulness, typically through a practice of meditation, contributes to overall well-being. In 2014, *Time* magazine called it "the mindful revolution."[13] Developing mindfulness is a great boost for effective reflection.

Jon Kabat-Zinn, a leading researcher and teacher in this field, explains that "[m]indfulness is *what arises when* you pay attention, on purpose, in the present moment, non-judgmentally, and as if your life depended on it."[14.]

Because of its potential to help us know ourselves, destress, and be intentional about our actions, many workplaces have incorporated mindfulness training into their development programs. Perhaps the most well-known is Google's Search Inside Yourself (SIY) program, started in 2007 by one of Google's engineers, Chade-Meng Tan. He brought together experts in mindfulness techniques, neuroscience, leadership, and emotional intelligence to develop a course for Google employees. There was so much demand for the program that in 2012, Meng and collaborators spun it off into a nonprofit institute (SIYLI.org) that now offers mindfulness training in 50 countries.[15]

There are many accessible options for exploring mindfulness and what it could mean for you, including apps, books, and courses that can help you get on the path of quieting your mind, awakening to the present moment, and developing greater compassion for yourself and others. You just need to take the first step.

▶ **GIVE YOURSELF CREDIT FOR WHATEVER YOU ARE ALREADY DOING**

Most likely, you don't have to start from scratch. You may already have established some habits that prompt you to reflect—even if you don't label them as such.

When asked, Fellows can recall many times when they've paused in their daily routines to think. Some keep a gratitude journal, or they take time each evening to consider what they have accomplished during the day and identify priorities for the next one. One Fellow said that every day when he pulls out of the driveway on his way to work, he stops for a minute to think about what he will focus on during the day.

Runners say that they choose to run without headphones and music just so they can have quiet time to think. Some dog walkers do the same.

For others, sitting quietly with a cup of coffee in the morning, with no cell phone in sight, before the rest of the family is up, gives them a peaceful moment to be with their thoughts.

The cumulative benefits of these practices can be substantial—if we take time to connect the dots. Haruki Murakami, the renowned Japanese novelist, did that in his memoir, *What I Talk About When I Talk About Running.* "Most of what I know about writing, I've learned through running every day," he wrote. Running prompted him to ponder how much he could push himself, how much rest he needed, how much he should focus on the world outside and how much on his internal world, when he should be confident or have self-doubts. Finally, he concluded, "I know that if I hadn't become a long-distance runner when I became a novelist, my work would have been totally different."[16]

It behooves each of us to consider when, in our days filled with work and family commitments, we are already taking a few minutes to think. These habits can serve as a foundation for building a more robust reflection practice.

▶ KEEP A JOURNAL

When First Movers arrive at the first seminar of the Fellowship, we give each a journal. They take notes as we move through the sessions. And we frequently give them journaling prompts and set aside time for them to write in their journals.

This journal becomes a record of their experience as a Fellow. If they use it consistently in and between seminars, it becomes much more. It documents their growth as a leader of change. It captures the fateful questions they are grappling with. It chronicles the learnings they have received from conversations with other Fellows and with people in their own companies as they engage with them to imagine innovations that will improve the business value and society.

Establishing a consistent journaling practice can deliver multiple benefits.

To learn about how to begin and get a glimpse of the payoffs, you can reliably turn to Julia Cameron's *The Artist's Way: A Spiritual Path to Higher Creativity*. Published originally in 1992, the book is now available in its 30th anniversary edition.

Its focus on spirituality may be off-putting for some, but the basic principles are universally applicable. At the heart of Cameron's approach are two tools. The first she calls "the morning pages." It requires writing three pages of stream-of-consciousness thoughts in longhand every day. The second is "the artist date," during which you set aside about two hours a week to nurturing your "creative consciousness." It can be an excursion to a museum, a walk, or a visit to an unfamiliar church. But you must do it by yourself.[17]

Cameron explains that this is a "two-step, two-directional process" and likens it to a radio receiver and transmitter. "Doing your morning pages, you are sending—notifying yourself and the universe of your dreams, dissatisfactions, hopes. Doing your artist date, you are receiving—opening yourself to insight, inspiration, guidance."[18]

Cameron's objective is to help you ignite your creativity. Others write of the business-oriented benefits of journaling. Eric McNulty, associate director of the National Preparedness Leadership Initiative, also advocates journaling with pen and paper and believes the practice can make you a better leader. "Setting aside as little as 10 minutes a day to record your thoughts," he writes, "stimulates reflection critical to making sense of the fast-moving world around you, which is, in turn, essential to effective leadership."[19] His practice includes monthly goal setting, ongoing reflection on his personal manifesto, and his plans for the coming week. He also takes time to write down three or four things he is grateful for each week.

Crafting your own strategy for journaling will help you get started and set a rhythm for writing subsequent journal entries.

▶ TAKE A WALK BY YOURSELF OR WITH OTHERS

Ryan Holiday, who has written extensively on the relevance of stoicism for our times, is an advocate for taking daily walks. He cites the walking habits of many philosophers, musicians, and reformers and notes that it is "a paradox that perhaps the single best way to still one's mind is to put the body in motion."[20]

In *Meditation for Beginners*, Jack Kornfield writes about a "walking meditation" as a way to practice mindfulness. He suggests walking in a place already familiar to you—even within your home—so that you are not distracted by new sights. Take tiny steps and focus on lifting your foot, placing it down, lifting the other foot, placing it down.[21] This action will help you become centered on the present.

We build time for walks into our agendas for Fellows because we understand how refreshing they can be. Sometimes the walks are completely unstructured. Sometimes we pair Fellows and offer a question to spark their conversations. During the pandemic lockdowns, we had Fellows pair up for a phone call while each walked on their own.

Rahul Raj, on the First Movers design team, created a "conscious constitutional." Each Fellow was invited to go on a walk, carrying their journal and an envelope that contained several smaller envelopes. They were told to leave their house and walk in the direction they take least often. After about five minutes, they were asked to find a spot where they could sit and open envelope number one. There they found a slip of paper with a reflection prompt. In one of these walks, the prompt was to think about what was troubling them that day or making them anxious. We suggested that the Fellows write their thoughts in their journal. They continued on their walk and opened the remaining envelopes as they went. Toward the end, they were prompted to address a challenge that many of us face: trying to do too much. They were asked to write a "not to do" list in their journal. The final envelope contained a quote that Fellows could reflect on as they walked home.

You can easily create a conscious constitutional for yourself by collecting reflection prompts and heading off, with journal in hand, in the direction that you take least often. After five minutes of walking, find a spot that makes you happy and where there is room to sit. Once you're comfortable, open envelope number one and begin.

Or skip the envelopes and set out with the intention of turning your work into a "microadventure," as Jancee Dunn suggests. Pay attention to scents along the way, be on the lookout for wildlife, or take a walk in the rain or fog.[22]

▶ READ POETRY

In the previous chapter, I wrote about the importance for First Movers of daring and learning to give voice to their values. In my early days at the Aspen Institute, I recall having a small moment of daring myself: I slipped a poem into an agenda I was crafting for a convening of senior leadership development experts. Looking back, it hardly seems like a courageous act, more like a small bet, but it felt pretty daring to me at the time.

Here is how it happened. Shortly after coming to the Institute after nearly two decades as a banker, I had responsibility for designing an agenda for a multiday convening with this group. We were gathering to discuss what kind of leaders we needed in business to ensure that the decisions they made considered impacts on all their stakeholders—not just their shareholders. (We hosted these meetings over several years, and these rich discussions eventually led us to launch the First Movers Fellowship Program.)

I distinctly remember the moment when I decided to introduce a poem into one of the sessions in that agenda. It was a poem by Mary Oliver called "The Journey." I had no idea how people would react. Poetry had certainly never been featured in meetings at the bank where I had worked, so I was far from practiced at the art of facilitating such a discussion. But working at the Aspen Institute, with its explicit focus on reflection, gave me cover. The poem was a hit. It triggered a fresh and meaningful discussion and opened space for a heartfelt conversation.

I believe it was at the moment I decided to go for the poetry that I truly stepped into my role at the Aspen Institute and left behind the constraints I had felt in my previous jobs. Since then, I have selectively used poetry in many of the meeting agendas I have designed.

So in 2009, when I had the opportunity to work with an amazing design team to create the First Movers Fellowship Program, poetry felt like a must. Over the years, design team member Dave Sluyter, who had used poetry extensively in his work at the Fetzer Institute and beyond, has helped introduce us to evocative poems for our seminars, and he has often facilitated the discussions.

The Fellows have enjoyed reflecting on poems in the seminars so much that they started a poetry circle among themselves and have maintained it for over a decade. Members periodically select a poem to share with the email group and offer a few questions to prompt reflection. Each year, more Fellows join the group.

If we give poems our full attention, they can change the way we see ourselves and the world around us; and the language, so compact, stays with us long after we have put the poem aside.

If you are not already a poetry reader, you may be unsure how to find poems that hold meaning for you. One source for suggestions is the Poetry Foundation (poetryfoundation.org). It is a treasure trove. Also, the Academy of American Poets offers a free subscription service that brings a poem a day to your electronic mailbox (poets.org).

Every bookstore has a small selection of poetry books. Make it a habit when you wander through the shelves to see which poets each shop has chosen to display.

If there are children in your life, ask a librarian or the owner of your local bookstore for a recommended selection of poetry, and try reading a few poems with your sons or daughters, nieces or nephews. It's no mystery why children love the poems of poets like A. A. Milne, Nikki Grimes, and Shel Silverstein. Read them aloud and wait for reactions.

You might also begin a practice of asking friends to send you their favorite poems. You may be surprised how many you receive and how enjoyable it is to read a poem with your friend in mind.

▶ GO OUTSIDE

To encourage reflection, we host seminars in a conference location with access to outdoor space. When we meet in the Aspen Institute's conference facility in Colorado, we are surrounded by mountains; in rural

Maryland, we are near the Chesapeake Bay; and in Tucson, we meet near a canyon filled with stately saguaros. These are spectacular backdrops for reflection. However, you don't have to travel to exotic locations to find what poet Wendell Berry calls "the peace of wild things."[23]

Take advantage of whatever outdoor space is available to you. A small garden or green space can calm the mind and provide a space for reflection. Oliver Sacks, the fabled psychiatrist, wrote of the calming and healing power of gardens. Not only did they spark his own creativity, but he observed that they also had a salutary effect on his patients. "In 40 years of medical practice," he wrote, "I have found only two types of non-pharmaceutical 'therapy' to be vitally important for patients with chronic neurological diseases: music and gardens."[24]

Next time you want to calm down so that you can think, simply try going outside.

▶ GET LOST

As you embark on your reflection journey, don't be afraid to get lost. This advice comes from Bruce Mau, a pathbreaking Canadian designer who works on huge projects around the world designed for social impact.

Mau learned the importance of this principle early in life. He grew up in the Canadian north, in a house on the border of what he calls a "boreal wilderness." He often explored the forest that stretched for hundreds of miles beyond his house. Mostly those excursions went well, but on a couple of occasions he felt the "gut-wrenching confusion" of losing his way. When that happened, he recounts, hypervigilance kicked in. He found his way home and realized the profound joy of recovery. No GPS for him.

That experience explains why "Think like you are lost in the forest" is one of the 24 design principles that have guided his work for decades, as he describes in his book *Mau MC24*.[25] The value of this principle wasn't immediately apparent to me; but as I read further, I began to grasp the idea that getting lost is essential for any entrepreneurial designer and, it seems, for anyone who wants to make big change.

"Once you realize you're truly lost," Mau writes, "you develop acute vigilance—you're attentive to every detail of everything that surrounds you. More than that, you spontaneously engage in critical analysis."

Reflection, as I mentioned earlier, allows you to take time to consider the choices you have made in life and the actions taken in the context of your personal purpose and aspirations. And it helps you see what you need to do in the future to align with your hopes and dreams.

But reflection can also make you feel lost. It can take you out of your comfort zone when you realize that you have wandered off your intended path or that the path you had chosen isn't leading you in the right direction. It's then that Bruce Mau's advice comes in handy. Lean into the acute vigilance that feeling lost can bring. Look within this disorienting forest for greater insights—and clarity about where to head next.

Then think of the words of William Faulkner, "You cannot swim for new horizons until you have courage to lose sight of the shore."

Building a reflection practice can help you gain that courage to swim in the direction of a new horizon. It can also help sustain you as you travel the path of a corporate social intrapreneur. That journey can bring both challenges and triumphs, but reflection can serve as a compass along the way.

Before enlightenment, chop wood, carry water.
After enlightenment, chop wood, carry water.

—ZEN BUDDHIST PROVERB

CHAPTER 12

Persist on Your Journey

When I began writing a book for corporate social intrapreneurs, I sought the advice of many friends and colleagues. By great good fortune, Betty Sue Flowers was among those who generously shared insights.

Betty Sue's diverse accomplishments include editing the fabled PBS interview series that Bill Moyers conducted with Joseph Campbell, *The Power of Myth*. Myths, Campbell explained, reveal to us the universality of the hero's journey, a story told in every spiritual tradition and in much of the literature, art, and films that elevate our understanding of the human condition.

What Betty Sue helped me see was that the story of corporate social intrapreneurs is a hero's journey as well, and she recommended that I approach the book with this perspective in mind. As I delved more deeply into the experiences of intrapreneurs, I realized the wisdom of that advice.

Like the heroes in oft-told tales, many intrapreneurs I know received a call to adventure. It took the shape of striving to find a way to work more purposefully with a result that benefited their companies, people, and the planet. To triumph, these heroes needed to confront the forces of greed, profit maximization at all costs, inertia, conflicting priorities, discrimination, and corporate reorganizations. And they had to slay their own internal dragons as well—the voices in their heads that told them they didn't have the time, strength, authority, or wisdom to go against these forces arrayed against them.

In mythology, heroes may resist the call to adventure initially and refuse to accept its burden but in time decide to set out on the path. Along the way, they encounter many obstacles, meet enemies and allies, and undergo multiple ordeals. If they are lucky, they receive the guidance of mentors (their personal Yodas) who help them prevail. Eventually, they return from their journeys with an "elixir," often in the form of enhanced knowledge or a breakthrough strategy, that enriches the community from which they came. Even if their journey has not been fully successful, they return a changed person for all they have learned along the way. They are ready to step up to the next challenge.

Similarly, the corporate intrapreneur's journey can result in significant victories, but there are always additional challenges ahead. Changing entrenched corporate cultures, established ecosystems, and short-term-oriented metrics used to define business success requires time and faithful perseverance. That is why the final chapter of this book is called "Persist on Your Journey" rather than something like "Cross the Finish Line" or "Celebrate Success." The appropriateness of that choice was confirmed for me when I reached out to First Movers and asked them what advice they would offer for those who wish to work as corporate social intrapreneurs.

Many responses were along the lines of the note sent to me by Jimena Garcia, now the vice president of marketing for Sonova Group, who said, "Make sure that you have a clear vision and that you are resilient. Set a clear path to get to your vision, but pivot when need be. Engage the right stakeholders and define your early wins so you get better buy-in from the organization. The path is not going to be easy, but don't give up!"

In my conversations with nearly 300 Fellows over 15 years, I have learned about the trials they faced on their journeys, what kept them going, and how they overcame obstacles along the way.

Time and again, I have heard from marathoners, like Yolanda Malone and Toni Ballabriga, whose stories are illustrative of the persistence of many.

Yolanda's Journey

Yolanda Malone's decades-long career as a packaging engineer started in a lecture hall at Michigan State University (MSU). Entering MSU in the 1980s, she had planned to be a computer science major but was dissuaded when she realized that she would end up working in back rooms with punch cards. That isolation wasn't for her.

So she started exploring other fields where she could use her love of science and math. By chance, she attended a Packaging 101 lecture given by a legendary MSU professor, Theron "T" Downes. "He showed us the essential role that packaging plays in our lives," Yolanda recalled. "Everything we purchase needs packaging to protect it before it reaches the consumer." (Just think of how you get five pounds of flour home from the grocery store or a bottle of mouthwash home from the pharmacy or how these items arrive on your doorstep if you order them online.)

Yolanda was intrigued by the combination of creativity and science required to thrive in that profession. She also liked the fact that the department had an internship program that gave undergraduate students real work experience along with their classes. By the end of the lecture, she was hooked.

For more than 30 years, she never looked back. Working at Johnson & Johnson, Nabisco, Conagra, and PepsiCo, she helped develop packaging for iconic products from Tylenol to Oreo and LifeSavers to Lay's potato chips. Until her recent retirement, she had global responsibility for designing and executing the packaging strategy for PepsiCo's food brands.

But her chosen profession presented challenges she couldn't have anticipated years ago in that college classroom. "Midway into my career," she told me, "I recall listening to a speaker who highlighted the many headwinds consumer products companies would soon face. These forces—like water scarcity, climate change, and changing consumer expectations—would have huge impacts on our business. I realized then we had to look far over the horizon to address big trends but do so in smart, incremental ways that took us in the right direction. It was a huge new professional challenge for me."

Even as sustainability became a significant priority for PepsiCo, Yolanda constantly confronted challenges that complicated the company's aspiration "to build a world where packaging never becomes waste" and to do so in a way that ensured that all packaging would protect and preserve the product and appeal to customers. When she started her career, she knew she had to design packaging that got a product safely to a customer. But as her career evolved, she realized that she must also design for the "end of life" of a package, to take responsibility for what happens after the consumer eats or drinks the product and throws the container away.

Consider, as one example, what it takes to create a compostable package, as PepsiCo did for its Off the Eaten Path plant-based snacks.[1] "Standard flexible packaging has been developed over decades and is very reliable," Yolanda explained. "Now we have to completely redesign this packaging so that when it is discarded, it turns into water and CO_2."

Few of us realize that flexible packaging for many of the food products we enjoy consists of multiple layers of film. To be compostable, each layer must be reengineered to decompose in diverse soils. The layers also have to accept printing inks, seal properly, and keep out oxygen and moisture so that the product stays fresh. Yolanda's team designed and ran multiple pilots to test ideas. "We did small batches to catch major problems as we went," she said. "A failure would send us back to the drawing board with valuable knowledge about what doesn't work. And then we would set off again on the journey, armed with new insights."

Getting the technology right is challenging, but it is just the starting point. No company can develop sustainable packaging without regard for the enormously complex food and waste system in which it is a part. Yolanda had to understand and navigate the expectations and limitations of many players in the system, including other consumer goods companies, vastly different municipal waste systems across the U.S. and other countries where PepsiCo sells products, and varying state and country regulations regarding waste. "On top of that, we had to consider the motivations of the for-profit waste haulers and the willingness and ability of consumers to recycle," she noted. Expectations of all these groups are rarely fully aligned. So Yolanda was constantly learning, cajoling, and course-correcting when required.

Always top of mind for Yolanda was the PepsiCo consumer. She constantly considered what that consumer wanted and could afford to pay. She also was determined to make it much easier for them to recycle, compost, or reuse the packaging materials that arrived with PepsiCo products.

"Throughout my career at PepsiCo, when I worked on packaging solutions," Yolanda said, "I always thought about my relatives. I come from a family of very limited means. My grandmother had a ninth-grade education and spent every day selling Stanley Home Products to have enough income to support her husband and their kids. I want her and those like her to be able to afford and enjoy PepsiCo products. So packaging has to achieve sustainability objectives but not lead to an increase in the price of the product or impair its ease of use. When I go to family reunions with my cousins, I want them to have a pantry full of products I've worked on." Aspiring to meet the needs of these customers—and millions of other hardworking families—kept Yolanda on her journey.

In her career, she also faced personal challenges. As a woman of color, Yolanda had to demonstrate over and over again her ability to perform against her peers. "It's frustrating," she said, "to be rated as highly as a white male colleague who gets promoted two years before you do, or to be told you have to prove this or that far more often than a peer—and then your manager changes, and you have to start again."

Fortunately, PepsiCo recognized Yolanda's talent and her passion for moving to a new, sustainable frontier in packaging. In return, throughout her years at the company, Yolanda imagined and created innovative packaging solutions for this global brand.

Toni's Journey

Antoni "Toni" Ballabriga's call to adventure as an intrapreneur came shortly after he joined BBVA, one of Spain's largest banks, in September 2007. Trained in corporate social responsibility (CSR), Toni felt well prepared to take on the role of director in BBVA's responsible business practice.

He hadn't anticipated a global crisis that would shake the entire financial system and lead to a massive recession and widespread hardship across the world. By 2012, the unemployment rate in Spain, his home country, would reach 25 percent.

Toni quickly realized that established CSR practices would be woefully inadequate for the seismic upheavals facing banks, governments, and the public around the world.

BBVA's solvency during this protracted crisis was never in doubt, but it was clear to Toni that BBVA could not simply stay the course and ride out the turbulence. Public trust in financial institutions was sinking. Banks around the world were being shored up and not held accountable, enraging a public that blamed them for practices that led to the crisis and cost people their homes and their jobs.

"I knew we had to do business differently, and I had the opportunity to help the bank rethink the way it needed to change. I realized my job was to break comfort zones within the bank, to have uncomfortable conversations and ensure that consideration for the impacts that the bank had on people's lives were fully embedded in our decision-making."

As the crisis deepened, Toni aimed at something so seemingly mundane that it had escaped the notice of many. He sought to change the way BBVA communicated with its customers.

Toni believed that banks had contributed to a decline in trust by offering customers overly complex financial services and documentation filled with impenetrable language. So he launched an effort within BBVA to ensure that the bank's communications and relationships with customers in all of the countries where BBVA had offices reflected what came to be called "Transparent-Clear-Responsible" (TCR) practices.

The task was daunting. It required multiple initiatives through the bank—in advertising and commercial documentation, customer relations and legal contracts. Hundreds of employees had to be involved in creating and vetting new approaches. Toni designed a two-year work plan and built a team of colleagues to review the bank's advertising code, write a corporate glossary, develop a communications manual for customer relations, and set new legal guidelines for contracts. Every contract for individuals and businesses was reviewed for compliance with the new guidelines. Procedures for opening accounts and applying for credit were streamlined, and response times were reduced. And along the way, the team sought advice, counsel, and buy-in from the bankers who worked with clients.

The work took years, but TCR is now standard procedure in the bank's operations across the globe, and it is a core component of its value proposition. The results of this project show up in positive customer satisfaction and trust scores. As Toni said, "TCR was a great example of what we do as social intrapreneurs. We create organizational kinetics from a peripheral position. And we always need to think big to evolve to the next level, the next challenge."

By 2015, the global financial crisis had subsided, but that year Toni was called to accept another adventure. He distinctly remembers the confluence of three events: The United Nations Sustainable Development Goals were defined and approved. Terms of the Paris Agreement were agreed to at COP21, the UN Climate Change Conference. And Mark Carney, then governor of the Bank of England and chairman of the Financial Stability Board, delivered an unforgettable speech, titled "Breaking the Tragedy of the Horizon—Climate Change and Financial Stability." Speaking to central bankers, supervisors, and insurance experts, with words that rang out to players across the financial industry, Carney warned that if action on climate wasn't taken immediately, by the time it became a defining issue for financial stability, it might be too late.[2]

"Climate change and sustainability was not only a financial risk but also the biggest business opportunity for banks," Toni recalled. "It was time for massive change, a total transformation in the bank." And he knew he could step up, with support from like-minded executives, to lead the bank toward a new strategic vision, one that fully embedded sustainability. "We had to change ourselves, and we had to help our clients transition to a more sustainable world," Toni said. "So in 2018 we created our Pledge 2025 to commit to mobilize €100 billion from 2018 to 2025 to support climate initiatives and inclusive growth, not through philanthropy but through the business model itself."

Only 18 months later, the bank took a significant additional step and included sustainability as core to its strategy. Sustainability became "business as usual." Toni realized that he had succeeded when in a leadership meeting the board chairman told everyone, "This is not going to be Toni's issue anymore; this is your issue." In the new strategic plan, the sustainable finance goal increased to €300 billion, and the bank committed to achieve net-zero greenhouse gas emissions in their lending and investment portfolios, in accordance with the most ambitious scenario of the Paris Agreement.

Even with all these commitments, Toni still finds himself pushing for bolder changes than others want. Recently, for example, he was the only person in a senior leadership meeting advocating for more stringent metrics for meeting net-zero targets for an industry group served by the bank. Others favored a less disruptive approach. After several months of negotiations, the bank accepted Toni's proposal.

In addition, seeing the need for transformative change within the entire financial industry, in 2018 Toni decided to take his intrapreneurial spirit outside the bank. "I knew we needed new rules for the financial system and that BBVA should play an active role in building a new architecture for the industry. It was an aha moment when I noticed that I should work not only at BBVA, but also from BBVA, for this systemic change."

Since then, Toni has become cochair of the global steering committee within the United Nations Environment Program–Finance Initiative (UNEP FI). He is also on the steering committee for the Net Zero Banking Alliance, and he chairs the Sustainable Finance Expert Group for the European Banking Federation.

In these roles, working with an array of bankers across multiple institutions in dozens of countries requires him to employ practices used by intrapreneurs the world over: deep listening to the perspectives of others; reframing problems; finding common ground; and holding fast to the principles, purpose, and vision that prompted him to choose this journey in the first place.

Toni told me that one of the quotes that inspire him to persist on his journey is from Gonzalo Muñoz, the UN Climate Change High-Level Champion from the COP25 Presidency: "The race to net zero and against climate change will not be won when the first arrives at the finish line, but when the last crosses it." Toni is committed to doing what he can to bring others across that line.

Choosing to Embark on Your Own Intrapreneurial Journey

Yolanda and Toni have demonstrated persistence on their intrapreneurial journeys, keeping lofty goals in sight even when they could only glimpse success on the far horizon. Many others have done the same.

But I know that many of you reading this book may wonder if you are ready to accept the call to this kind of professional adventure.

Taking on one more responsibility when you are already stressed by all you have to do can feel like a burden too much to bear. Better just to keep your head down and carry on with your assigned tasks. Moreover, you may ask yourself, "How can I make meaningful change in my organization, anyway? Wouldn't I be taking on a Sisyphean task, destined to push a huge rock up the hill, only to have it roll down again, time after time?"

You may also have doubts that you are up to the task: "Am I really the one to take on this battle? Do I have the skills and the wisdom not only to see possibilities that others miss but then to act on that vision? And if I head in this direction, will there be anyone willing to accompany me on the journey? Maybe I can leave it to others to move first, and then I can get on board."

These personal factors—lack of time, self-doubt, and fear of isolation—are amplified by organizational realities that make it difficult for corporate social intrapreneurs to triumph. You may worry that arguing in favor of innovations is a losing battle against entrenched norms and practices.

If the system seems stacked against you, it's understandable that you may resist the call to adventure, to blaze into the white space and find opportunities at the intersection of business success and social progress.

But for those of you eager to link your desire to make a difference with the many skills you bring to your work, I hope that the stories in this book will give you courage to step forward and the strategies will give you confidence to persist.

A growing number of people are accepting the call to be social innovators within their companies. But we need even more to step up. This book will serve its purpose if, after reading it, you accept the challenge and feel better prepared to work in a way that allows you to love your job and live your purpose.

To close, I want to tell a story not from the world of First Movers, but from literature. I think it inspires all who seek to make possibilities a reality and change business for good.

In 1988, Paulo Coelho, a Brazilian novelist, published *The Alchemist*, the story of a young shepherd who sets off in search of treasure that he has seen repeatedly in his dreams. As the shepherd continues on his journey, Coelho writes, "before a dream is realized, the Soul of the World tests everything that was learned along the way. It does this not because it is evil, but so that we can, in addition to realizing our dreams, master the lessons we've learned as we move toward that dream. That's the point at which most people give up."[3]

To find the treasure, Coelho says, you must keep going even when the light dims and the path is blocked. For those dreamers who persist, Coelho has encouraging words: "When you want something, all the universe conspires in helping you to achieve it."[4]

In a television interview with Oprah Winfrey in 2014, Coelho revealed that when *The Alchemist* was first published, it didn't sell, and his publisher dropped it. These results were disappointing, but Coelho believed in his book and was determined to live by the words he had written.[5] So he persuaded another publisher to pick it up. Shortly thereafter, when 500,000 copies had been sold, Coelho asked the publisher why he had agreed to take this chance. The publisher said he really didn't know. He just did it. In the television interview, Oprah suggested that what happened was fate, and Coelho agreed. The universe was helping him out.

The Alchemist has now sold over 65 million copies and has been translated into 80 languages.

For all of you corporate social intrapreneurs, take heart. Don't give up. Wait for the light. You might even look to the universe to give you a boost. By accepting the call to adventure and setting out on your arduous journey, you will be helping companies realize their potential for making a positive impact in the world. And you will be blazing a path for other intrapreneurs to follow.

You will also find that you are doing work that matters—to you, to your company, and to society.

"Thank you" is the best prayer you can say.
I say that one a lot. Thank you expresses
extreme gratitude, humility, understanding.

— ALICE WALKER, FROM INTERVIEW IN
CIRCLING FAITH: SOUTHERN WOMEN ON SPIRITUALITY

Acknowledgments

How far back should one go in recognizing those who contributed in so many ways to the writing of a book? I want to start 25 years ago when I met Judy Samuelson through a mutual connection. At that time, Judy had just left the Ford Foundation and was starting a program focused on the role of business in society that eventually became the Aspen Institute Business & Society Program. She has been executive director since its inception. She took a bet on me in 2000 and offered me a role in this new organization. After my years in banking, I felt that I had finally come to a place where I could do my best work, where I could do work that mattered. Judy made that possible by giving me space to imagine and create. When I dreamed of launching the First Movers Fellowship Program, she offered her full support and has continued to champion this work for over 15 years. I can't say enough about how much her trust and guidance have empowered my work—and led me to this book.

An amazing design team has helped the Fellowship Program—and this book—become a reality. At the outset, in addition to Judy, the design team included Matthew Breitfelder, Shari Cohen, Fred Dust, Mary Gentile, Sarah Rienhoff, and David Sluyter. Many are still contributing in important ways to the Fellowship Program. Joe Brown, Lohen Parchment, Rahul Raj, and Rachel Wheeler have now joined the design team and are adding their wisdom to the program design and execution. I am especially grateful to Eli Malinsky, another design team member and gifted colleague, who expertly took over from me as director of the First Movers several years ago. Other dedicated design team members over the years have included Garrett Barr, Rachel Botos, Anita Dumas, Danielle Holly, Suzanne Howard, Trisha King, and Bryan Walker. These fellow travelers have left indelible marks on the Fellowship. And they have inspired, encouraged, and taught me in ways too numerous to mention.

Of course, the book would not exist without the accomplished and purpose-driven First Mover Fellows, who have made the program come alive. Their commitment to doing work that matters and to the Fellowship is inspiring. I am so grateful to those who gave me permission to share their stories in this book. There are so many other stories waiting to be revealed. I wish I could have included them all.

Over the years, I have also benefited from the wisdom and support of many others who have been generous with their help and guidance and have been champions for this work. They include Elisa Alt, Mariana Amatullo, Michael Barnett, Adrienne Brodeur, Jerry Davis, Betty Sue Flowers, Ante Glavas, Julia Kirby, Steffen Landauer, David Langstaff, Mary McBride, Krishen Mehta, Claire Preisser, Maureen Scully, Deborah Siegel, Linda Wells, Christopher White, and Boniface and Alison Zaino. A special thanks to Niko Canner, who has always been available to offer insights, and to Dorothy "Dee" Dunn, who has been a believer in the First Movers Fellowship even before it took shape. And when I had doubts that the book would ever be finished, Dee helped reignite my commitment to move forward.

There are many others whose insights and research I have referenced throughout the text whose work has been foundational for my own.

In the process of writing, I was extraordinarily lucky to have two insightful and knowledgeable editors: Fran Smith and Elissa Rabellino. The book is immeasurably better because of their help. I am also grateful for the opportunity to work with Sasha Wizansky, who designed the book and its evocative cover.

In 2018 I was honored to be selected for the residency program at the Rockefeller Foundation's Bellagio Center and had the extraordinary privilege of spending four weeks at the center in Italy. There I could devote full days to finishing an early draft of this book. It has evolved considerably since then, but having that dedicated time to consolidate notes into a coherent whole was a true gift. I also benefited from being in conversation with other accomplished and thoughtful residents with widely diverse perspectives who helped me think more deeply (and more critically) about the role that business plays in society. I am so grateful for this experience.

Finally, the process of writing this book has been a very long one, and I am enormously appreciative of friends and family members who have consistently prodded and encouraged me, offered critical insights, and expressed ongoing interest in the book as it emerged. In particular, I want to thank Robert Campoy and Erin Ballard for generously sharing their design expertise. Finally, I want to express special gratitude to my husband, who has been an unwavering, patient champion and helpmate along this lengthy book-writing journey. Thank you!

Endnotes

CHAPTER 1

1   Samuel J. Palmisano, "The Globally Integrated Enterprise," *Foreign Affairs*, May/June 2006.

2   Robert E. Kelley, *How to Be a Star at Work: 9 Breakthrough Strategies You Need to Succeed* (New York: Three Rivers Press, 1999).

3   Drucker Institute, "Opportunity in Disguise," January 14, 2011, https://drucker.institute/news-post/opportunity-in-disguise/.

4   Edelman, *2022 Edelman Trust Barometer*, https://www.edelman.com/trust/2022-trust-barometer.

5   United States Environmental Protection Agency, "Facts and Figures about Materials, Waste and Recycling—Textiles: Material-Specific Data," epa.gov, https://www.epa.gov/facts-and-figures-about-materials-waste-and-recycling/textiles-material-specific-data#TextilesOverview.

6   Gerald F. Davis and Christopher J. White, *Changing Your Company from the Inside Out: A Guide for Social Intrapreneurs* (Boston: Harvard Business Review Press, 2015).

7   Rosamund Stone Zander and Benjamin Zander, *The Art of Possibility: Transforming Professional and Personal Life* (New York: Penguin Books, 2002), 21.

CHAPTER 2

1   Nick Craig, *Leading from Purpose: Clarity and the Confidence to Act When It Matters Most* (New York: Hachette Books, 2018), 3.

2   Naina Dhingra, Jonathan Emmett, Andrew Samo, and Bill Schaninger, "Igniting Individual Purpose in Times of Crisis," *McKinsey Quarterly*, August 18, 2020, https://www.mckinsey.com/capabilities/people-and-organizational-performance/our-insights/igniting-individual-purpose-in-times-of-crisis.

3   Bill George, *Discover Your True North, Expanded and Updated Edition* (Hoboken, NJ: John Wiley & Sons, Inc., 2015), 1.

4   Simran Jeet Singh, *The Light We Give: How Sikh Wisdom Can Transform Your Life* (New York: Riverhead Books, 2018), 219.

5   Brené Brown, *Dare to Lead: Brave Work. Tough Conversations. Whole Hearts.* (New York: Random House, 2018), 187–91.

6   Nick Craig, *Leading from Purpose: Clarity and the Confidence to Act When It Matters Most* (New York: Hachette Books, 2018), 36.

7   Hal Gregersen, *Questions Are the Answer: A Breakthrough Approach to Your Most Vexing Problems at Work and in Life* (New York: Harper-Business, 2018), 268.

8   Gregersen, *Questions Are the Answer*, 272–73.

9   Tim Urban, "Inside the Mind of a Master Procrastinator," TED Talk, 2016, https://www.ted.com/talks/tim_urban_inside_the_mind_of_a_master_procrastinator/c.

10 Annie Dillard, *The Writing Life* (New York: Harper & Row, 1989).

CHAPTER 3

1   Information about this project is available at Clean Team Ghana, www.cleanteamtoilets.com.

2   https://www.epa.gov/facts-and-figures-about-materials-waste-and-recycling/food-material-specific-data

3   Information about Appreciative Inquiry is available at the Cooperrider Center for Appreciative Inquiry at Champlain College, https://appreciativeinquiry.champlain.edu/.

CHAPTER 4

1   http://www.clifbar.com/stories/sustainability-certifications-and-seals

2   https://walmart.cexchange.com/online/home/index.rails.

3   Michael E. Porter and Mark R. Kramer, "Creating Shared Value," *Harvard Business Review*, January–February 2011, https://hbr.org/2011/01/the-big-idea-creating-shared-value.

4   David Packard, *The HP Way: How Bill Hewlett and I Built Our*

Company (New York: Harper Business, Collins Business Essentials, 2006, reprint ed.).

5 This video offers an introduction to the work HP did with the Clinton Health Access Initiative (CHAI): https://www.youtube.com/watch?v=lgpCrtyhyeA.

6 Business Roundtable, "Business Roundtable Redefines the Purpose of a Corporation to Promote 'An Economy That Serves All Americans,'" August 19, 2019, https://www.businessroundtable.org/business-round-table-redefines-the-purpose-of-a-corporation-to-promote-an-econo-my-that-serves-all-americans.

CHAPTER 5

1 Karl Weick, "Small Wins: Redefining the Scale of Social Problems," *American Psychologist* 39, no. 1 (January 1984): 40–49.

2 Chip Heath and Dan Heath, *Switch: How to Change Things When Change Is Hard* (New York: Broadway Books, 2010), 44.

3 Heath and Heath, *Switch*, 124–48.

4 Weick, "Small Wins," 43.

5 Weick, 43–44.

6 https://www.statista.com/statistics/870924/worldwide-digital-trans-formation-market-size/#statisticContainer

7 BCG, "Flipping the Odds of Digital Transformation Success," BCG. com, October 29, 2020, https://www.bcg.com/publications/2020/in-creasing-odds-of-success-in-digital-transformation.

8 United Nations, Climate Action, "Water—at the Center of the Climate Crisis," https://www.un.org/en/climatechange/science/climate-is-sues/water#:~:text=Climate%20change%20is%20exacerbating%20both-,world's%20water%20in%20complex%20ways.

9 American Water Works Association, "Dawn of the Replacement Era: Reinvesting in Drinking Water Infrastructure," May 2021, https://www.awwa.org/Portals/0/AWWA/ETS/Resources/DawnReplacement-Era.pdf.

10 Heath and Heath, *Switch*, 141.

CHAPTER 6

1   Peter Guber, "The Four Truths of the Storyteller," *Harvard Business Review* (December 2007), 53–59.

2   Carmine Gallo, *The Storyteller's Secret: From TED Speakers to Business Legends, Why Some Ideas Catch On and Others Don't* (New York: St. Martin's Press, 2016), 17.

3   Lin-Manuel Miranda, "Commencement Speech—University of Pennsylvania, May 16, 2016," https://www.youtube.com/watch?v=e-wHcsFlolz4.

4   International Labour Organization, *Lured by a Job, Trapped in Forced Labour*, video, created by the CGF (Consumer Goods Forum) and the ILO, https://www.ilo.org/global/about-the-ilo/multimedia/video/public-service-announcements/WCMS_235344/lang--en/index.htm.

5   Chip Heath and Dan Heath, *Made to Stick: Why Some Ideas Survive and Others Die* (New York: Random House, 2007).

6   Mario Juarez, "Try These Six Techniques and Be a Storytelling Master," January 31, 2022, Mario-Juarez.com, https://mario-juarez.com/new-blog/2019/7/30/try-these-six-techniques-and-become-a-story-master.

7   Gallo, *The Storyteller's Secret*, 7.

8   Margaret Renkl, interview, *PBS NewsHour*, April 22, 2022, https://www.pbs.org/newshour/show/margaret-renkl-writes-about-the-environment-from-her-blue-dot-hometown-in-red-state.

CHAPTER 7

1   Amy Edmondson, "How to Turn a Group of Strangers into a Team," TED Salon, https://www.ted.com/talks/amy_edmondson_how_to_turn_a_group_of_strangers_into_a_team.

2   Bill Gates, "Can the Wi-Fi Chip in Your Phone Help Feed the World?" *GatesNotes*, October 9, 2018, https://www.gatesnotes.com/FarmBeats?WT.mc_id=10_11_2018_07_FarmBeats_BG-LI_&WT.tsrc=BGLI&linkId=58042336.

3   Amy C. Edmondson, "The Three Pillars of a Teaming Culture," *Harvard Business Review*, December 17, 2013, https://hbr.org/2013/12/the-three-pillars-of-a-teaming-culture.

4   Deborah Ancona and Hal Gregersen, "How to Cultivate Leadership That Is Honed to Solve Problems," *strategy+business*, October 30, 2017, https://www.strategy-business.com/article/How-to-Cultivate-Leadership-That-Is-Honed-to-Solve-Problems.

5   Ancona and Gregersen, "How to Cultivate Leadership That Is Honed to Solve Problems."

6   Ancona and Gregersen.

CHAPTER 8

1   Hal Gregersen, *Questions Are the Answer: A Breakthrough Approach to Your Most Vexing Problems at Work and in Life* (New York: Harper-Business, 2018), 13.

2   Edgar H. Schein, *Humble Inquiry: The Gentle Art of Asking Instead of Telling* (Oakland, CA: Berrett-Koehler Publishers, Inc., 2013), 2.

3   Schein, *Humble Inquiry*, 4.

4   Jacqueline M. Stavros, Lindsey N. Godwin, and David L. Cooperrider, "Appreciative Inquiry: Organization Development and the Strengths Revolution," in *Practicing Organization Development: Leading Transformation and Change*, 4th ed., eds. William J. Rothwell, Jacqueline M. Stavros, and Roland L. Sullivan (Hoboken, NJ: John Wiley & Sons, 2016).

5   Diana Whitney, Amanda Trosten-Bloom, David Cooperrider, Brian S. Kaplin, *Encyclopedia of Positive Questions: Using Appreciative Inquiry to Bring Out the Best in Your Organization*, 2nd ed. (Brunswick, OH: Crown Custom Publishing, 2013), 2.

6   Whitney et al., *Encyclopedia of Positive Questions*, 17.

7   Whitney et al., 39.

8   Whitney et al., 89.

9   Warren Berger, *A More Beautiful Question: The Power of Inquiry to Spark Breakthrough Ideas* (New York: Bloomsbury, 2014), 8.

10 Berger, *A More Beautiful Question*, 25.

11 Gregersen, *Questions Are the Answer*, 12.

12 Krista Tippett, *Becoming Wise: An Inquiry into the Mystery and Art of Living* (New York: Penguin Books, 2016), 110.

13 Alison Wood Brooks and Leslie K. John, "The Surprising Power of Questions," *Harvard Business Review*, May–June 2018, 60–67.

14 Michael Bungay Stanier, *The Coaching Habit: Say Less, Ask More, and Change the Way You Lead Forever* (Toronto, ON: Box of Crayons Press, 2016).

15 Gregersen, *Questions Are the Answer*, 67–74. Gregersen also describes the process in a short YouTube video: https://www.youtube.com/watch?v=ATFxGSywAcU.

16 Nilofer Merchant, "To Change Someone's Mind, Stop Talking and Listen," *Harvard Business Review*, February 6, 2018, https://hbr.org/2018/02/to-change-someones-mind-stop-talking-and-listen.

CHAPTER 9

1 Nancy Kline, *More Time to Think: A Way of Being in the World* (Pool-in-Wharfedale, England: Fisher King Publishing, 2009), 34.

2 Mark Goulston, *Just Listen: Discover the Secret to Getting Through to Absolutely Anyone* (New York: American Management Association International, 2010), 59.

3 Merchant, "To Change Someone's Mind, Stop Talking and Listen."

4 Dan Kim, "Delivering Decarbonized Transport," *Yale Insights*, March 2, 2022, https://insights.som.yale.edu/insights/delivering-decarbonized-transport.

5 Goulston, *Just Listen*, 4.

6 Kate Murphy, *You're Not Listening: What You're Missing and Why It Matters* (New York: Celadon Books, 2020), 17–18.

7 Stephen R. Covey, *The 7 Habits of Highly Effective People: Restoring the Character Ethic* (New York: Fireside/Simon & Schuster, 1990), 241.

8 Caren Osten, "Are You Really Listening, or Just Waiting to Talk?," *Psychology Today*, October 5, 2016, https://www.psychologytoday.com/us/blog/the-right-balance/201610/are-you-really-listening-or-just-waiting-talk.

9   Sherry Turkle, "Stop Googling. Let's Talk," *New York Times*, October 5, 2016, https://www.nytimes.com/2015/09/27/opinion/sunday/stop-googling-lets-talk.html.

10 Covey, *The 7 Habits of Highly Effective People*, 245.

11 Henry David Thoreau, "Life Without Principle," *Atlantic Monthly*

12, issue 71 (October 1863): 484–95, https://www.thoreau-online.org/life-without-principle.html.

CHAPTER 10

1   https://www.linkedin.com/pulse/social-intrapreneurs-reca-librate-your-inner-compass-maximum-bhargava/

2   More information about Mary Gentile, PhD, and Giving Voice to Values is available at https://givingvoicetovaluesthebook.com/about-mary.

3   An online course, Ethical Leadership through Giving Voice to Values, taught by Mary Gentile, is offered by the University of Virginia on Coursera, https://www.coursera.org/learn/uva-darden-giving-voice-to-values. (The course is free to audit. There is a fee to take the course interactively and get a certificate.) The seven pillars are presented in this video: https://www.coursera.org/lecture/uva-darden-giving-voice-to-values/the-seven-gvv-pillars-JInrE.

4   Mary Gentile, *Ways of Thinking About Our Values in the Workplace* (Darden Business Publishing, University of Virginia, 2010), https://store.darden.virginia.edu/ways-of-thinking-about-our-values-in-the-workplace.

5   Shelly L. Francis and the Center for Courage & Renewal, *The Courage Way: Leading and Living with Integrity* (Oakland, CA: Berrett-Koehler Publishers, 2018), iBooks.

CHAPTER 11

1   Tchiki Davis, "Self-Reflection: Definition and How to Do It," Berkeley Well-Being Institute, https://www.berkeleywellbeing.com/what-is-self-reflection.html.

2   Howard Gardner, *Extraordinary Minds: Portraits of 4 Exceptional Individuals and an Examination of Our Own Extraordinariness* (New York: Basic Books, 1997), 146.

3   James O'Toole, *The Executive's Compass: Business and the Good Society* (New York: Oxford University Press, 1993).

4   The Aspen Institute, "A Brief History of the Aspen Institute," https://www.aspeninstitute.org/about/heritage/.

5   Jennifer Porter, "Why You Should Make Time for Reflection (Even If You Hate Doing It)," *Harvard Business Review*, March 21, 2017, https://hbr.org/2017/03/why-you-should-make-time-for-self-reflection-even-if-you-hate-doing-it.

6   Tim Kreider, "The 'Busy' Trap," Opinionator, *New York Times*, June 30, 2012, https://archive.nytimes.com/opinionator.blogs.nytimes.com/2012/06/30/the-busy-trap/.

7   Neil Pasricha, "This Two-Minute Morning Practice Will Make Your Day Better," *Harvard Business Review*, January 22, 2021, https://hbr.org/2021/01/this-two-minute-morning-practice-will-make-your-day-better?autocomplete=true.

8   Thich Nhat Hanh, *Your True Home: The Everyday Wisdom of Thich Nhat Hanh* (Boston: Shambhala, 2011), Practice 287.

9   Judy Brown, *A Leader's Guide to Reflective Practice* (Bloomington, IN: Trafford Publishing, 2008), 23.

10 Marshall Goldsmith, "6 Questions That Will Set You Up to Be Super Successful," MarshallGoldsmith.com, July 20, 2015, https://marshallgoldsmith.com/articles/6-questions-that-will-set-you-up-to-be-super-successful/.

11 Muriel Wilkins, *Coaching Real Leaders*, podcast, HBR, https://hbr.org/2020/12/podcast-coaching-real-leaders.

12 Joseph L. Badaracco, *Step Back: How to Bring the Art of Reflection into Your Busy Life* (Boston: Harvard Business Review Press, 2020), 3–11.

13 Kate Pickert, "The Mindful Revolution," *Time*, January 23, 2014, https://time.com/magazine/us/1543/february-3rd-2014-vol-183-no-4-u-s/.

14 Jon Kabat-Zinn, *Mindfulness for Beginners: Reclaiming the Present Moment—and Your Life* (Boulder, CO: Sounds True, 2012), 17.

15 More information about Chade-Meng Tan's work is available at Chade-Meng Tan, *Search Inside Yourself: The Unexpected Path to Achieving Success, Happiness (and World Peace)* (New York: HarperOne, 2012).

16 Haruki Murakami, *What I Talk About When I Talk About Running*, trans. Philip Gabriel (New York: Alfred A. Knopf, 2008), 81–82.

17 Julia Cameron, *The Artist's Way: A Spiritual Path to Higher Creativity, 10th Anniversary Edition* (New York: Jeremy P. Tarcher/Putnam, 1992, 2002), 9–20.

18 Cameron, *The Artist's Way*, 18.

19 Eric J. McNulty, "Journaling Can Boost Your Leadership Skills," *strategy+business*, May 15, 2018, https://www.strategy-business.com/blog/Journaling-Can-Boost-Your-Leadership-Skills.

20 Ryan Holiday, "The Life Changing Magic of Taking a Long Walk," *Thought Catalog*, November 12, 2018, https://thoughtcatalog.com/ryan-holiday/2017/11/the-life-changing-magic-of-taking-long-walks/.

21 Jack Kornfield, *Meditation for Beginners* (Boulder, CO: Sounds True, 2004), 74.

22 Jancee Dunn, "How to Make Your Walk a 'Microadventure,'" *New York Times*, June 23, 2023, updated July 3, 2023, https://www.nytimes.com/2023/06/23/well/move/walk-microadventure.html?searchResultPosition=2.

23 Wendell Berry's poem "The Peace of Wild Things" is available in multiple collections, including Wendell Berry, *The Peace of Wild Things* (New York: Penguin Books, 2018), 25.

24 Oliver Sacks, "The Healing Power of Gardens," *New York Times*, April 18, 2019, https://www.nytimes.com/2019/04/18/opinion/sunday/oliver-sacks-gardens.html.

25 Bruce Mau, *Mau MC24: Bruce Mau's 24 Principles for Designing Massive Change in Your Life and Work* (New York: Phaidon Press, 2020), 230–41.

CHAPTER 12

1 https://www.pepsico.com/our-stories/press-release/frito-lay-launches-industrially-compostable-bags-with-off-the-eaten-path-brand-a09232021

2 Mark Carney, "Breaking the Tragedy of the Horizon—Climate Change and Financial Stability," speech given at Lloyd's of London, September 29, 2015, https://www.bankofengland.co.uk/speech/2015/breaking-the-tragedy-of-the-horizon-climate-change-and-financial-stability.

3 Paulo Coelho, *The Alchemist*, trans. Alan R. Clarke (New York: HarperCollins, 1993), 139.

4 Coelho, *The Alchemist*, 23.

5 Oprah Winfrey, "Oprah Learns the Secret to Paulo Coelho's Timeless Wisdom," Oprah.com, 2014, https://www.oprah.com/inspiration/oprah-talks-to-the-alchemist-author-paulo-coelho/all.